D0507439

Education and Racism

Education and Racism is a concise and easily accessible primer for introducing undergraduate and graduate students to the field of race and education. Designed for introductory courses, each chapter provides an overview of a main issue or dilemma in the research on racial inequality and education and the particular approaches that have been offered to explain or address them. Theme-oriented chapters include curriculum, school (re)segregation, and high-stakes testing, as well as discussions on how racism intersects with other forms of marginality, like socio-economic status. The focus on particular educational themes is the strength of this book as it paints a portrait of the systematic nature of racism. It surveys multiple approaches to racism and education and places them in conversation with one another, incorporating classical as well as contemporary theories. Although conceptually rich and dense with critical perspectives and empirical study, the book uses clear and transparent language throughout for easy comprehension.

Perfect for courses in Multicultural Education, Sociology of Education, Ethnic Studies and more, *Education and Racism* is the ideal primer for engaging students new to race and education without sacrificing the content for those who are already familiar with the field.

Zeus Leonardo is Associate Professor of Education and Affiliated Faculty of the Critical Theory Designated Emphasis at the University of California, Berkeley.

W. Norton Grubb is Professor Emeritus, David Gardner Chair in Higher Education Emeritus, and Program Coordinator, Principal Leadership Institute, at the University of California, Berkeley.

Education and Racism

A Primer on Issues and Dilemmas

Zeus Leonardo and W. Norton Grubb

Routledge
Taylor & Francis Group

NEW YORK AND LONDON

CONCORDIA UNIVERSITY LIBRARY
PORTLAND, OR 97211

First published 2014
by Routledge
711 Third Avenue, New York, NY 10017

Simultaneously published in the UK
by Routledge
2 Park Square, Milton Park, Abingdon, Oxon OX14 4RN

Routledge is an imprint of the Taylor & Francis Group, an informa business

© 2014 Taylor & Francis

The right of Zeus Leonardo and W. Norton Grubb to be
identified as authors of this work has been asserted by them in
accordance with sections 77 and 78 of the Copyright, Designs
and Patents Act 1988.

All rights reserved. No part of this book may be reprinted or
reproduced or utilized in any form or by any electronic,
mechanical, or other means, now known or hereafter invented,
including photocopying and recording, or in any information
storage or retrieval system, without permission in writing from
the publishers.

Trademark notice: Product or corporate names may be
trademarks or registered trademarks, and are used only for
identification and explanation without intent to infringe.

Library of Congress Cataloguing-in-Publication Data
Leonardo, Zeus, 1968–
Education and racism : a primer on issues and dilemmas / by
Zeus Leonardo and W. Norton Grubb.
pages cm
Includes bibliographical references and index.
1. Racism in education–United States. I. Title.
LC212.2.L457 2014
370.8–dc23
2013010785

ISBN: 978–0–415–89100–4 (hbk)
ISBN: 978–0–415–89101–1 (pbk)
ISBN: 978–0–203–81437–6 (ebk)

Typeset in Garamond and Officina Sans
by Keystroke, Station Road, Codsall, Wolverhampton

Printed and bound in the United States of America by Publishers Graphics,
LLC on sustainably sourced paper.

Table of Contents

Preface

As a textbook, the following explication aims to familiarize, in more or less simple terms, the rather complex challenges that educators face with respect to honoring diversity in schools in the United States and maintaining equity at their center. Its concerns and context are U.S.-specific so the book reflects issues associated with this focus. It is not designed as a "kitchen sink"-type book that introduces in comprehensive fashion the history of race and education. By and large, these books already exist. The current book and authors have other ambitions and provide descriptions for novice educators, or those uninitiated in the field, who will benefit from a brief introduction to racism in education as it manifests itself in particular practices and school structures. We accomplish this by keeping the explanations conceptually rich and the perspectives critical.

Each chapter provides an overview of a main issue or dilemma in the research on racial inequality and education, and the particular approaches that have been offered to explain or address them. Thus, it is theme- rather than group-oriented. The book's organization comprises a chapter on each of the following: curriculum, cultural relevance, school–community relations, school (re)segregation, funding and resources, and high-stakes testing. It does not proceed by focusing on specific populations and their group experience with education, such as African Americans, Latinos, or Asian Americans. Rather, each chapter emphasizes an educational issue, for which research on these minority populations provides the evidence that racism is a formidable force in education. We provide these specific group experiences where they illuminate the themes under study.

We frame these issues as they have been studied by a range of scholars coming from diverse perspectives on the problem of racism in education, but favor the anti-racist implications of multiculturalism. Multiculturalism is the most established framework for addressing racism in education, but rather than focusing on its promotion of diversity in schools, we emphasize its links with anti-racist education. We believe this comes with the advantage of posing the problem of racism as the main obstacle to transcend. The book is practical in tone, but uses research-based arguments. It applies conceptual frameworks to explain the nature of racial inequalities without assuming too much research background on the part of its readers. It uses simple explanations without oversimplifying the issues. Combining theories and empirical studies allows us to recruit diverse explanatory frameworks to explain the phenomenon of education and racism.

Focusing on particular educational themes or aspects enables the book to offer descriptions of how racism appears in discrete areas of schooling as well as specific explanations about why these areas develop the way they do. This is done in order to paint a systematic or institutional portrait of racism and how it pervades the entire school experience. As much as possible, we provide portraits of the race forest as well as the trees. Although we certainly do not exhaust the arenas wherein racism appears in schools, we argue that it is reproduced across the structure of education from curriculum decision making, to resource allocation, to testing practices. Isolating any one of these themes in education will be limited in its ability to apprehend the seriousness and depth of racism in schools. Moreover, changes in one facet of schooling are likely to produce effects in other realms, some of which are unintended. Furthermore, these dimensions reinforce each other, such as when resource depletion is felt across the curriculum or endangers supports for students of color who speak languages other than English. Therefore, a multi-pronged problem deserves a multi-dimensional analysis.

The book is designed as a primer, an *essential*, which means that it takes on a particular appearance. Within each chapter, multiple subheadings signal transitions between internal points regarding the educational phenomenon under study. For example, in Chapter 1 on curriculum, subheadings link curriculum development with questions around transformation of the canon of dominant readings, history revision, and the politics of knowledge, summed up with the provocation, "What knowledge is of most worth?" In Chapter 4 on school segregation, subheadings provide interconnections among tracking practices, the racialized distribution of information, and the unrealized goal of and continued search for integration. At the end of each chapter, study questions are designed to provoke readers into critically reflecting over their own sites and contexts to locate racism where it occurs, determine the practices that undergird and maintain it, and formulate strategies to ameliorate it. All chapters end with suggested readings for future study, as a way to develop a knowledge base for understanding education and racism.

The following is an outline of the book's chapters, organized under specific themes.

Chapter 1: Curriculum and Racism

This chapter introduces what has become the most widespread approach to examining racism and education. Since the early 1970s, writings from the founders of multiculturalism, such as James Banks, Carl Grant, and later Sonia Nieto and Christine Sleeter, argued for a broadening of the well-acknowledged Eurocentric curriculum. In particular, this curriculum movement aimed to change the "canon" in order to include the voices, knowledge base, and perspectives of minorities. Curriculum transformation came into prominence in the 1990s when the "culture wars" in education broke out of the academy and influenced society at large. Defenders of the Western canon responded to curriculum reform by reasserting the "tried and true" knowledge of Eurocentrism. A couple of decades later, multi-culturalism has become common sense as most, if not the majority, of schools have incorporated the mission of diversity into their curriculum. This chapter documents the history of curriculum reform as an educational intervention into racial inequality, the importance of knowledge relations, and how race relations became a battleground to distinguish between the knower and the objects of knowledge.

Chapter 2: Culturally Relevant Education and Racism

From the perspective of many minority groups, schooling has become largely irrelevant to their culture, understanding, and belief systems. In short, despite the efforts of minority scholars, teachers, and reform movements, education does not reflect their worldview and racial inequality continues under the guise of universal education. This means that children of color experience schooling as largely foreign to their self-concept, a process that neither affirms nor is ultimately useful to them. Nowhere is this more poignant than in the education of English Language Learners. This chapter documents the research and writing on the cultural divide between school knowledge and minority groups. Schooling is shrouded within the cloak of Whiteness, which becomes the unquestioned way that schooling, even with the existing challenges of multiculturalists, proceeds. The writings in Culturally Relevant Pedagogy and its main proponents, such as Geneva Gay and Gloria Ladson-Billings, have tried to address this culture gap. Now one finds books and articles on culturally relevant mathematics education, literacy, and the like. That said, the formidable challenge of making education and school knowledge relevant to students of color continues.

Chapter 3: School–Community Relations and Racism

Most educators will admit that a positive relationship between schools and communities forms part of a solid foundation for a child's schooling. For families of color, their "funds of knowledge" are not recognized, and a certain incongruence develops between their family/community and schools. Often, families of color are rendered invisible through discourses of deficiency. Their potential contributions to schools are ignored as they are frequently depicted as a "problem" or hurdle to achieving excellence; here excellence is opposed to diversity or equity, rather than building the notion that schools cannot be excellent as long as they only consider seriously the contributions of mainstream families. Students of color experience "subtractive schooling" as their communities become marginal to the official school culture. Racism becomes a form of neglect as schools not only assume the passivity of communities of color, but actively encourage it. Nowhere has this been more documented than in the differential experiences of parents of color whose involvement has not been cultivated. Critical educators have tried to dispel this image with narratives about community empowerment and more accurate portrayals of communities of color. Critical scholars remind schools of the agency within communities of color.

Chapter 4: Tracking, Segregation, and Racism

One of the most pronounced ways that second-generation segregation is enacted in schools is through the practice and naturalization of tracking, which is the focus of this chapter. The literature on tracking strongly suggests that schools promote an intellectual division of labor, which then reproduces the wider division of labor in the workplace. Reproduction Theory was largely a class-based argument that schools reproduce the division of labor required by capitalism. This chapter argues that racial reproduction in schools also happens alongside class reproduction. With the dominance of tracking in U.S. schools, few people can imagine either a time of schooling that existed before tracking or the possibilities of de-tracking (mixed-ability classes) in the future. Yet tracking produces very predictable and unequal results for minority groups, particularly Latinos and Blacks. In effect, where racial groups meet in a school context, we have a "two-school" phenomenon wherein Whites and Asian Americans have upwardly mobile educational experiences, whereas Latinos and Blacks find themselves in lower tracks where they and their teachers have both lower social status and less access to higher-status knowledge. This chapter examines how tracking is one of the main structures for reproducing racial hierarchies in schools.

Chapter 5: Funding, Resources, and Racism: When Money Matters

Not only are students of color defined in ideological terms, but they are also targets of material disparities in funding and resources, the concern of this chapter. Because of the way that educational policies, like Proposition 13 (1978) in California, for example, are structured, schools that serve dispro-portionate numbers of students of color in urban districts—frequently poor areas—suffer in terms of never having either enough or appropriate school materials. In other words, they lack the very things that facilitate the educational process; e.g., books, acceptable facilities, and adequate teaching and school accessories. This chapter takes on a "more resource" approach to suggest that students of color are victims of resource inequities as well as ideological forms of racism. Documented spectacularly by Kozol's *Savage Inequalities* (1991), students of color attend schools that are the shell of such institutions. Facilitated by laws and funding policies, and supported by ideological understandings of "deserving or not deserving," the resource deprivation in these schools mimics the actual condition of their neigh-borhoods: ghettoized, dilapidated, and abandoned. Although Culturally Relevant Pedagogy and other such attempts to raise the social status of people of color may go a long way, it cannot be accomplished without a simultaneous redistribution of resources. In short, students of color suffer both dispossession, a resource form of racism, and dishonor—its ideological form—in schools.

Chapter 6: High-Stakes Testing, Accountability, and Racism

High-stakes testing, particularly in the U.S. context, has been the main concern of educational reform since the early 2000s. If we place it within the larger phenomenon of standardization in education, then its history is even longer. Its most common, yet controversial, form is the federal act of 2001, No Child Left Behind (NCLB). There has been much research on the deleterious effects of NCLB as it concerns school-aged children of color, from the more benign-seeming effect of making demands without appropriate funding to the more nefarious consequence that implicitly blames them for their own "failures." This chapter takes up the racial ramifications of high-stakes testing. It takes up the way in which initiatives like NCLB, while recognizing students of color as a subgroup, fundamentally minimize the structure of race as playing a determining factor in their life chances.

Chapter 7: Education and Racism: Future Directions

This chapter ties the themes together with respect to orientations, paradigms, and ways of framing the problem that may ameliorate racism in education. By way of concluding, it argues that racism in education is a structural problem at the heart of the enterprise of schooling, reflected in many deeply rooted practices. Although the chapters offer a careful look at the particular aspects of the process, this chapter asserts that changing one at the expense of the others does not go far enough in addressing the structural nature of racial inequality. We argue that a "composite picture" of racism in education benefits educators, particularly pre-service teachers. Moreover, racism in education is structural in another sense. It is part of a larger social problem of racial disparities that link schooling with the functioning of the economy, housing, status relations, and the like. In other words, although educators may go a long way to address school phenomena by targeting certain practices and traditions within education, this cannot be accomplished in isolation from a broader understanding of education as a node within a larger framework of institutional racism. In a sense, school reform is bound up with social reform in general.

There are many aspects of schooling that are laudable and the socialization of young people is one of its important functions. In advanced Western societies, such as the United States, the common schools of the mid-1800s began what we now know as education's current form. It serves many purposes, such as vocational training, cultural participation, citizenship, and social integration. But the creation of schools also happened in the context of what most educators would acknowledge as a deeply racialized society. We are referring, of course, to slavery. Today, enslavement is part of our national past, but it appears that racism is not, which forms the crux of our arguments throughout this book. To the extent that racism remains a stubborn part of our present, we hope the analysis we put forth sheds light on it.

Reference

Kozol, J. (1991). *Savage inequalities*. New York: Harper Perennial.

Introduction

Education and Racism

Pedro prepares for school on this partly cloudy, partly sunny day in Los Angeles, California. After finishing his breakfast, he brushes his teeth and dresses in his low-rise jeans and black T-shirt with "Che" emblazoned on its chest. He does not really know much about Che Guevara, the Argentinian revolutionary socialist leader. He wears the shirt because it is at once colorful and "tough"-looking at the same time. He laces his skate shoes, puts his backpack on, kisses his Puerto Rican mother, and rides his skateboard. His father, a Salvadoreño immigrant, is already at work. Pedro physically looks racially ambiguous, Latino to some, Black to others. He is bilingual in English and Spanish, but he and his friends speak to each other mostly in English. He likes going to school, a place where some kids share similar interests with him, such as skateboarding. When he arrives at school, his friends, mostly Latino and Black, greet him at the steps leading up to the main gate. They give each other the "fist pound" and raucously enter the school grounds together. Most of Pedro's friends are in the basic track, enrolled in classes that are not designed to prepare them for four-year college experiences later.

At 15 years old and a high school sophomore, Pedro is in a mix of class levels, college-prep for mathematics and English and a smattering of basic courses in science and others. Like most kids, Pedro does not love studying and would rather be at the mall or skate park, but he does well in school, though his parents believe he could be doing better. In many respects, Pedro is a well-adjusted kid, growing up in a lower middle-class home with two incomes, with parents who emphasize the importance of education and put a lot of trust in his teachers. His parents are workers, the father in construction, the mother a restaurant cashier. They speak English but are

Spanish-dominant. Having saved money for about 10 years, they recently purchased a modest house with three bedrooms and have three children; Pedro is the eldest and shares a bedroom with his siblings. The paternal grandmother lives with them. Pedro experienced a Catholic education up until high school and with tuition money freed up, his parents could afford a house in a mostly Latino neighborhood, otherwise known as a barrio. The parents attend some school events, such as parent–teacher conferences, but in general, they have faith that the teachers are looking out for their son's best interests. They also rely on Pedro to be an intermediary between school and home, often translating information for them.

Pedro's first period after homeroom is English where the curriculum consists of mostly readings from American literature, such as John Steinbeck's *Of Mice and Men* and Toni Morrison's *The Bluest Eye*. All of the books are in English as is the language of instruction. There are not enough copies of each book to go around so at any given point in the curriculum, half of the kids read one book while the other half of them read another. It makes for some complicated lesson plans, but the teachers are creative and plan accordingly. There is some racial mixture in Pedro's class, but his high school is made up mostly of Latino and Black students, serving the neighborhoods that reflect those demographics. The few White students are in the higher tracks or Advanced Placement (AP). Because the school is mostly Latino and Black, the higher-track classes are also populated with them and they learn certain abstract skills. The mathematics curriculum goes only as high as trigonometry, so students who want to study calculus to prepare for college entrance must do so at the local community college. There are hardly any American Asian students but for some Samoans and Cambodians; they are concentrated in the lower tracks where they learn basic skills through worksheets and basal readers to prepare them for standardized tests. Most of the teachers are White women who do not live in the area but drive in from nearby suburbs. Most of them have been teaching for five years or less. They make attempts to know the community, frequenting its restaurants and fraternizing with some of its members. But they live busy lives, many of them with kids of their own, so they mostly go from home to work and back.

In many respects, this story seems like a normal scene. A school with well-intentioned teachers, busy and trusting parents, kids at their appropriate developmental stages, is as "American" as schooling gets. The adults are overextended or overworked, while the kids are rambunctious. But there are clues that race is very central to this otherwise average day. Pedro's neighborhood is an outcome of racial segregation, an almost permanent fixture of American life. It produces segregated schools, and in places like Los Angeles and other urban districts, school finance is a function of the real-estate tax base. In fact, according to Kozol (1991), poorer neighborhoods devote a larger percentage of this money to public services, like fire departments, cutting further into the school budget. Although in Pedro's school one finds students of color in higher-track classes, their access to high-status knowledge, such as calculus (and beyond, such as advanced calculus), is limited as are the school materials to which they do have access. The curriculum includes a modicum of multiculturalism, and a respect for diversity forms part of the ethos, but there are subtle messages that the students' education quickly hits a ceiling as monolingualism is the official mode of instruction. These normal circumstances are anything but "normal" and the institutional racism that informs them often goes unnoticed and is part of business as usual.

Racism in education is a structured condition that many, if not most, students of color experience. As understood here, racism is an institutional relationship of power. It can be described by appealing to "racist attitudes," but a focus on attitudes does not explain how they limit the actual lives and choices of people of color. To understand this, a definition of racism in education has to bring to the forefront the structural dimensions that result in people of color's marginalization, limitations, and lowered chances for success in schools. It is based on the hierarchical social system of race, which is the valuation of social groups grounded on skin-color differences. Although all racial groups, such as Blacks and Whites, possess a range of skin tones within each group, race is the stratification of people based on their racial ancestry or lineage. This is different from "colorism," which is the idea that darker people *within* a racial group suffer skin-tone discrimination to lower his or her chances for success, including education.

Race is also different from ethnicity, which is associated with culture. In contrast, race is a social system based on physical markers, the primary form of which is skin color. Increasingly, scholars have noted the shift happening from *biological racism*, or the notion that groups retain immutable or genetic traits like intelligence, where Whites are judged to be smarter than other races, to *cultural racism*, or the notion that groups embody cultures that lead to their social outcomes, such as whether or not they value education. These developments notwithstanding, race as the problem of the color line, as Du Bois (1989/1904) once called it, is the dominant form that race takes in the United States.

It is helpful to define race as a social construction. By this, we mean that although physical differences among groups are a reality, race is a way to construct what they mean for the purposes of social organization. Just to take one example of race as a social construction, consider the phenomenon of segregation. As it concerns interracial relationships, the United States only recently dismantled anti-miscegenation laws that legally forbade interracial marriages between Whites and people of color, particularly White with Black, as late as 1967 in the *Loving v. Virginia* case. Anti-miscegenation helps construct ideas around pure races, justifying laws that prevent genetic mixing in order to preserve the White race's claims to superiority by keeping the races segregated at the level of intimate relationships.

In other social realms, segregating the races means building White neighborhoods and ghettoizing Blacks and other groups of color. In other words, ghettos from South Central Los Angeles to South Side, Chicago are created by Whites, not Blacks. From Whites' organized attempts to keep Blacks out of their neighborhoods, such as rioting or blockbusting, to the Federal Housing Administration's use of discriminatory mortgage lending systems, Black ghettos were literally constructed at the turn of the 20th century. Ghettos are not places where Blacks plainly prefer to live in order to be around each other. Rather, before the 1900s, racial concentration of Blacks by neighborhood was not as pervasive. Black ghettos were later fabricated by housing laws and White preferences, making their appearance today seem natural and predestined; that is, ghettos seem like they are not structured by race. They even appear like a permanent fixture of the Black landscape. While it is true that White ethnics, such as Jews, experienced ghettoization in places like New York, first, these were fleeting compared to the seeming permanence of Black ghettoization; and second, White ghettos did not house the majority of their ethnic members within the larger metropolitan area like Black ghettos do for Blacks. Housing segregation for Blacks is more intense.

From anti-miscegenation to housing, segregation continues into education. Because many children attend their neighborhood schools, Black children attend school with other Blacks, White children with other Whites.

Although valiant efforts to integrate U.S. schools are on the educational agenda, they have proved difficult without simultaneous success in integrating other social realms, such as the division of labor and redistribution of wealth. Although race is a social construction, even an invention, it becomes a reality for all Americans and its effects are real. One of its lynchpins is segregation, a process of separating the races from bedrooms to classrooms.

Racism does not affect only people of color because it influences their relationships with teachers and White students alike. Racism lowers the educational experience for everyone even if White students enjoy a lift over others in the process. Its social costs affect everyone even if the brunt of racism is incurred by people of color. In some sense, educators neither condone nor wish to participate in racism. Especially after the innovation of multiculturalism, teachers, the majority of whom are White, have become more sensitive to racial issues in schools. From curriculum formation to cafeteria talk, teachers' public understanding suggests that they value diversity in America's schools.

These intentions aside, racism continues to be a formidable force in students' lives and those of their families. In this book, we argue that diversity must be paired with a deep appreciation for and commitment to racial equity and anti-racism. Some forms of discrimination, like the division of labor, are not created by schools even if they may help to reproduce them. In general, U.S. schools support the economic structure of capitalism and become one of its functions by training the workforce it requires. Thus, it is hardly fair to hold educators responsible for fixing problems they did not create. However, there are education-specific practices in which educators participate on a consistent basis. We analyze six of these school structures in this book.

Some well-established school practices not only reproduce racial inequality, they may actively produce it. Understanding how school structures, belief systems, and practices produce racism is the goal of this book. Its objective is to outline thematically the dynamics of racism in schools and how they have an impact on the concrete lives of communities and students, specifically minorities, as well as to provide some ideas on how to counteract racial inequality. Racism has become an educational dilemma and we hope this book unveils its processes and contributes to decreasing it in schools.

Education and the Ideology of Color-Blindness and Post-Racialism

As educators forge ahead with tackling race and racism in schools, several challenges regarding race are important to keep in mind. In a famous and lyrical passage from *The Souls of Black Folk*, Du Bois (1989/1904) wrote:

> After the Egyptian and Indian, the Greek and Roman, the Tueton and Mongolian, the Negro is a sort of seventh son, born with a veil, and gifted with second-sight in this American world,—a world which yields him no true self-consciousness, but only lets him see himself through the revelation of the other world. It is a peculiar sensation, this double-consciousness, this sense of always looking at one's self through the eyes of others, of measuring one's soul by the tape of a world that looks on in amused contempt and pity. One ever feels his twoness,—an American, a Negro; two souls, two thoughts, two unreconciled strivings; two warring ideals in one dark body, whose dogged strength alone keeps it from being torn asunder.
>
> This history of the American Negro is the history of this strife— this longing to attain self-conscious manhood, to merge his double self into a better and truer self. In this merging he wishes neither of the older selves to be lost. He would not Africanize America, for America has too much to teach the world and Africa. He would not bleach his Negro soul in a flood of white Americanism, for he knows that Negro blood has a message for the world. He simply wishes to make it possible for a man to be both a Negro and an American, without being cursed and spit upon by his fellows, without having the doors of Opportunity closed roughly in his face.
>
> (Du Bois, 1989/1904, p. 5)

Written at the beginning of the 20th century, Du Bois' observations appear to be relevant at the beginning of the 21st century. Teachers would be wise to note that the color line that Du Bois warned about has only become more entrenched. Racism produces in Blacks the experience of double consciousness from the pressure of having to live in two worlds: one Black, the other White. According to this description, being Black becomes a burden within a U.S. democracy that fails to extend its privileges to people of color. However, having this liberty taken away from them, Blacks also experience the gift of second sight and see the United States for what it is, an expression of White racial power. Although Du Bois wrote almost exclusively about the Black experience, we imagine similar dynamics happening in other communities of color. In education, this twoness is on display when students of color enter schools with their own cultural understandings intact, but experience the imposition of White culture as the standard by which they are judged. To a great extent, this process escapes many White students and teachers, who do not register the racial tension because they represent the norm. Their orientation could be called color-blind, or the luxury to avoid understanding how race works.

We acknowledge that the end of Jim Crow arrangements, developments around immigration policy and citizenship, and multiculturalism in schools all speak to the strident march of educational and social progress. However, if U.S. education is "kinder," so has racism taken on a gentler form, no longer assuming the explicit or transparent relation of power that characterized previous eras, such as enslavement or colonialism. Most educators would label Jim Crow—the pre-Civil Rights race arrangement that legally protected White entitlements while subverting people of color's basic rights—as a racist institutional arrangement, discredited as it is today. But many would also avoid labeling current housing and school segregation as facets of a different kind of racism. In effect, racism in the United States has taken on a color-blind appearance, which characterizes the current era of race relations affecting education and governance of schools.

In schools and universities, color-blindness's most obvious target is affirmative action, or the remediation of race inequality through policies that consider the institutional effects of race in order to create a "level playing ground." It is under periodic attack and threat of erasure, interpreted as racial preferential treatment for people of color. For example, in 2003, the *Gratz v. Bollinger* Supreme Court case ruled that while allowing for race as a consideration for admissions at the University of Michigan, it was unconstitutional for the university to design a point system that would give minority applicants admission points over White applicants. It followed on the heels of the passing of Proposition 209 in California in 1996, effectively outlawing affirmative action in the state. Race-conscious education faces serious challenges in the era of color-blindness that considers race perspective as part of the problem rather than the attempt to understand the nature of the problem.

Whereas during the Jim Crow era, racial minorities and Whites needed no candle to see in the light of day the reality of racial stratification, the ideology of color-blindness is effective in masking racism through the encouragement of individualism and personal choice. It sometimes goes under the banner of "post-racial" thought, or the idea that race and racism in the United States are part of the past. In public discourse, the development of color-blindness and post-racialism makes it difficult to name the processes of racism if race is no longer presumed to matter. It becomes hard to track racial discrimination in education, health, and the criminal justice system if race is not allowed to enter the conversation, or if it is illegal for governmental agencies, like school systems and the health industry, to collect racial data. In fact, this was the design of the Racial Privacy Act of California in 2003, which would have prevented official agencies from being able to collect demographic information about their constituents. It failed to pass, largely due to the mobilization of two of the largest unions in the country: teachers and nurses.

Although we find problems in color-blindness and post-racialism, we do not wish to exaggerate their power and influence. For now, we suggest that it benefits educators to understand why these concepts have explanatory power, even seductiveness, for some Americans. Color-blind thinking assumes that if we do not make race matter in social life, then racism will disappear. It argues that the problem is thinking in terms of race itself, since we are all humans. Color-blindness is not literally the utter inability to see race, but to see it selectively to accomplish certain goals. By contrast, we suggest that institutional racism and specific practices are the likely culprits, which requires seeing race with both eyes open.

Most people would acknowledge that racism continues, but color-blindness would define it as individual acts of hatred, most commonly captured through images of extremists. It is not considered an integral part of the fabric of U.S. social relations, the nation's governance, and its policies. It is a local problem to which bad people are susceptible. In addition, racism is said to be multi-directional, not just from Whites to people of color, but equally from minority to Whites or among minorities. Racial inequality is usually reduced to attitudinal racism or prejudice, such as the use of stereotypes. At its most brazen, color-blindness deems people who think through race as themselves racist since they are blamed for continuing the rather antiquated notion of race. Again, the upshot is that racism is in people's heads, not in the way that institutions work to give Whites an advantage, such as tracking practices in schools. The solution, therefore, is less structural and more attitudinal adjustment, less institutional and more individual change. But racism seems more intransigent than that, affecting racial groups differently, and in the end, durable.

Racism within color-blind ideology is not really about racism as a social problem, but it is portrayed as a deviance from a norm assumed to be racially equal. Racism's root in group contestation between minorities and Whites fades into the background and in its place appears an explanation of individual choices, usually couched within a market language that increases consumer options. In effect, racism becomes outdated and White advantage no longer its symptom. In fact, the most common portrait of racism today belongs to Arab or Muslim faces, often equated with terrorism after the 2001 bombing of the World Trade Center. Although we do not focus on the experiences of Muslims and Arab peoples in this book, we recognize that U.S. race relations post-9/11 are decidedly different. A cursory look at the popular language of "national safety" and counter-terrorism, as well as the name change from the Immigration and Naturalization Service to the Bureau of Homeland Security support this view.

However, with respect to public schools, it seems that reform still revolves around the perennial achievement gap between Latinos/Blacks and Asian Americans/Whites. Therefore, we have good reason to concentrate on this particular racial divide. That said, that racial minorities function within a larger social system determined by the color line is becoming more difficult to assert in public life. To some, it has become passé. But as this book will make clear, racism is alive and well, inserting itself into the daily experience of students in public schools. From curriculum reform, to school financing, to standardized tests, racism is a debilitating force in their lives.

In education, there are many efforts to address the achievement gap (the acceptable term for the racial disparity). Blacks and Latinos are on the receiving end of the disparity whereas Whites and Asian Americans receive the benefits. This does not sit well with most educators, whose analysis deserves to be developed with more depth. We attempt to provide an alternative framework that puts this picture in focus, arguing for a thematic analysis of race and education within an institutional framework. Rather than a color-blind approach, we offer a color-conscious one.

The ideology of color-blindness represents a fundamental challenge to race-minded educators, making institutional race analysis seem all but out of sync with public school culture despite the fact that we have no shortage of data pointing to the reality of institutionalized racism. The default perspective has been to "fix" the problem, including its targets. As part of blaming the victim, minority children are perceived through a deficit perspective that frames them as passive recipients of educators' good intentions. To reiterate, minority communities are not without their own share of problems which contribute to certain difficulties, such as the persistence of a culture of poverty that ghettoization and racial isolation produce. Crime in these communities is a reality, violence reaches a crisis situation, and hopelessness threatens their very future.

We recognize these trends and how communities contribute to them, but argue that they are responses to a condition they did not, on balance, make or have the ability to control. These unhelpful behaviors confirm the limitations placed upon them by race structures rather than verify the suggestion that they created their own lot. They are responses to the dehumanization they face, desperate as some situations have become. Color-blindness constructs them as bad individual choices by self-made people. We encourage educators to reframe this tendency, without underestimating the difficulties. For example, without downplaying the disorganization and high rates of crime which students in ghettos or other urban settings face, and sometimes succumb to, educators are in a position to enter these communities as partners through trust building, reciprocity, and mutual commitment. Racism is formidable, but it is not indomitable.

In education, although initiatives recognize the race problem, they do so within a post-racial sensibility. These problems are acknowledged to exist and NCLB deliberately names the racial achievement gap. But in general, the gap is not regarded as a product of a social system structured by a racial hierarchy. Without an institutional perspective, the race problem becomes a symptom of the groups themselves. They are the problem to be solved, not the racial structure that produced them. Within post-racialism, racial analysis is deemed an unwise use of time at best or looking for excuses at worst. After all, NCLB has given minority communities and their schools the chance to succeed by the deadline of 2014. In the end, they, not structural racism, may be blamed for their own conditions.

Post-race analysis is therefore also a post-racism species of argument. Its poster child is none other than President Barack Obama, who is claimed by color-blindness as *de facto* proof that the centuries-old problem of racism has seen its final day, not only once, but for a second time, as Obama becomes not only the first black president, but a two-term commander-in-chief at that. As a belief system, both color-blindness and post-racialism articulate with institutions and become powerful forces in education and society at large. Although racism is a social problem, the solution offered is centered on individual choices. Although the problem is racial in nature, the solution is non-racial.

This book introduces central themes for thinking about and teaching race in education. It is designed to be a *primer* and efficiently moves the reader from one theme to the next. It does not introduce the reader to the debate as to whether or not racism exists in education. Based on evidence and explanations, we argue that racism exists, is a structured part of education, and represents a fundamental challenge to educators who care about diversity and equity in schools. However, we do not suggest that it is easy to stamp out. Rather, we offer descriptions and explanations as places to begin a process for thinking about racism and how it may be ameliorated, first through critical analysis and then through deliberate interventions. We favor an institutional perspective on racism, which explains the psychological effects of lowered teacher expectations as well as the social conditions that lead to minority students' underperformance, sometimes their failure. But providing a general analysis for racism does little to illuminate the actual mechanisms that make it possible and sustain it. To this end, we provide specific descriptions of racial practices in education. We believe this takes the focus away from individuals and toward schooling within an institutional perspective.

References

Du Bois, W. E. B. (1989). *The souls of black folk.* New York: Penguin Books. First published in 1904.

Kozol, J. (1991). *Savage inequalities.* New York: Harper Perennial.

Curriculum and Racism

Introduction to the Curriculum

Curriculum creation is arguably the most appropriate way to begin a discussion around education and racism. Because schools are ostensibly places where students daily study "something" for a given amount of time, curriculum represents the actual material that facilitates this interaction. To most educators, curriculum is comprised of the content usually organized around subject matter or disciplines. In short, it is the "stuff" of schools, which teachers structure into instructional units within a classroom context and which students attempt to master. In reality, curriculum is a broader concept than this simplification might imply because curriculum creation includes values and politics, such as which knowledge counts most and how it should function in society. Nonetheless, it serves our purpose of starting a conversation based on a generally agreed-upon definition of curriculum as the content that students study.

Curriculum selection overlaps with concerns regarding instructional delivery or administration—for example, at the district level—but it is conceptually distinct from teaching or leadership. Why district leaders choose certain materials as well as how teachers will deliver them are different issues from what education, as a larger field of study, considers is a worthwhile collection of knowledge. This set of facts and perspectives as well as what they exclude is then systematized into discrete units of learning. In Chapter 4, we discuss tracking practices, which come with curriculum differentiation for students assigned to various levels. In this chapter, we introduce curriculum as students' relationship with school knowledge and how the curriculum implicates race relations.

Racism in the curriculum is first and foremost a question of representation. Below, we discuss the finer nuances of the racial politics of representation. Here we are concerned with a more literal interpretation of representation guided by the question, "Are people of color there?" Without proper accounting for this question, finer-grained analyses of representation will not achieve traction, or worse, will become moot issues. So the most overt issue to resolve in challenging racism in the curriculum is driven by the need to include people of color at multiple levels. To an important degree, these changes have occurred, largely through decades of school reform. They lead to the ultimate goal of significant, rather than superficial, inclusion of minorities in the curriculum.

Curriculum formation is rarely a transparent process, often going through multiple deliberations and iterations before becoming accepted as an official set of documents, like textbooks. It is debated at every foreseeable level of education, from local to national, informal to formal. Although it is becoming rarer, at the local level, curriculum setting invites teachers and administrators' input on what is considered knowledge of most worth for student learning. At the national level, politicians, academics, interest groups, and economics enter the picture as broader debates surrounding the United States' global standing become important. In large trend-setting states, like California and Texas, curriculum is also big business as textbook publishers enter the equation.

Curriculum is clearly a political matter as forging it ebbs and flows with power élites. For instance, to take a few examples, when *A Nation at Risk* was commissioned under President Ronald Reagan's administration, a national debate was sparked regarding the kind of curriculum that would give the United States a competitive global edge at a time when Reagan considered that educational standards had fallen below acceptable levels. This included an emphasis on raising standards for mathematics and literacy. Under President George W. Bush, formal laws and initiatives, such as No Child Left Behind, drive what standard curricula look like in attempts to ameliorate achievement gaps, most of which is experienced by four subgroups: English Language Learners, students with disabilities, poor or working-class children, and racial minorities. Curriculum is at once a source of the problem, whereby its relevance for some students but not others facilitates or delays achievement, as well as a potential solution for educational dilemmas through school reform.

Although their influence on curriculum setting is steadily decreasing, curriculum scholars exercise influence on the national debate regarding the direction the curriculum should take. It is more than what kind of knowledge most counts, but what kind of children, or citizens to be more precise, schools are going to produce. For curriculum is not only about processing information, but processing people as well. From the individual 50 states to the nation-state, curriculum defines central aspects of the social function that schools serve for society at large. The curriculum has the tendency to reproduce existing social relations and arrangements, but it may also challenge them. With respect to race, this process also implicates the uneven achievement rates among the racial groups and what, if anything, is to be done about them.

There are many curriculum schools of thought. From child developmentalists, like G. Stanley Hall, who argue for the cultivation of the child's "inner self"; to social reconstructionists, like George Counts, who see schools as agents of social change, particularly for economic equality; to humanists, like William Torrey Harris, who emphasize mental discipline and the training of reason; to social efficiency advocates, like Edward Thorndike, who model schools after factories and seek to increase efficiency and reduce waste—curriculum has always been a battle ground. More recently, proponents of great or canonical books, like Mortimer Adler, would revisit the debate on the national curriculum to which students should be exposed. Multiculturalists, like James Banks, would question the core knowledge of U.S. schools based on the fact that the nation's demographic is represented by different racial groups and what this means for national interest. Although not all educators and politicians agree that knowledge relations explain the heart of schools, the sheer amount of political and economic investment in curriculum formation suggests that it is a significant arena for the aims and development of education.

Curriculum, Race, and Racism

Curriculum setting is related to the racial organization of schools. On the most obvious level, the content that students study relates to the intellectual grappling with the history of race and racism. For example, the way that school materials handle events, like the establishment of the U.S. nation through colonialism or the 250 or so years of enslavement, sends a message about the treatment of these topics, such as their importance and centrality. The amount of space these topics occupy within the curriculum, year in and year out, suggests the amount of serious study that educators and students spend on them. In addition, their connection with today's social structures may be highlighted, thus providing their continuity with current outcomes, or they may appear as snapshots in history and having little to do with today's conditions.

Setting curricular parameters is not just an issue of deciding which facts to choose and how they will be highlighted. Through fact selection, a racial order is made because students learn what race means in their lives by virtue of how knowledge is organized and then woven together to tell a story. In short, the relationship between curriculum and race is part of the forging of race relations by grappling with it, and not just a re-enactment of its history through books. The main problem we seek to explore in this chapter with respect to the curriculum is its capacity to make race intelligible and by doing so to become part of race as a knowledge relation. In the act of ordering information and narrating history, knowledge becomes racial and race becomes part of the system of knowledge. This implicates knowledge in the racial project, knowledge which is no longer innocent or waiting to be discovered. People do not recruit knowledge simply to make race known to themselves, but that knowledge itself is already racial. For example, when history textbooks construct knowledge about racism as mainly a problem of extremist hate groups, such as the Ku Klux Klan or neo-Nazis, they promote a way of knowing that neglects the general system of White advantage in law, business, and national governance. Knowledge selection tells the story of race.

Curriculum setting is part of race creation rather than merely reflecting it. It is not a mirror, but a prism that bends the story of race for particular reasons. Curriculum has the ability to recreate race because students read their existence into and through their textbooks. In other words, curriculum making is part of race making. It is not just a way to explain the dynamics of race relations, but a way to reinforce, sometimes challenge, it in the very act of explaining it. In the worst cases, curriculum further marginalizes racial minorities, adding to the social inequality they experience outside school. When their social existence and participation in curriculum forging are minimized, they experience the educational form of racism. Although curriculum on its own, and education for that matter, are not responsible for the myriad reasons that lead to high minority drop-out rates and underachievement, such as the division of labor, it stands to reason that students who do not see themselves reflected in the curriculum will not have an organic connection with schooling, and will perceive it as separate from their intellectual development. This kind of disconnection has far-reaching implications for the kind of education they experience.

Curriculum is part of race making because race is a learned social relation. As a "social construction," race is ultimately not about people's biological or genetic make-up, but how physical markers, such as skin color, are interpreted to mean something about human worth, intelligence, and respect. That is, skin color is transformed into a symbol that associates racial groups with characteristics that have little to do with the tone of their skin. These human evaluations are then organized into a hierarchical system wherein Whites are judged as superior to people of color. To the extent that the color of one's skin owes itself to biology, particularly the amount of melanin, race is the attempt to make unchangeable or immutable socially defined traits, like intelligence, and then inextricably link them with their phenotype.

As a social relation, race is an invention. It is not just the history of skin color. It is the ability to make this rather simple symbol meaningful and powerful. Skin-tone difference among people has always existed; race relation is precisely how this difference becomes the basis for social organization and group as well as individual worth. The way we use it here, race is a modern concept and its history is rather recent. Tension among groups has always existed, such as ethnic warfare, but they do not always take on a racial form. The groundwork for race was laid when Europe colonized the Americas, became institutionalized when chattel slavery became a U.S. industry, and was then codified in U.S. law in the 18th century. Among race scholars, there is general agreement that the creation of racial forms includes at least two processes: the law of immutability, applied to concepts like intelligence; and the significance of skin color as an organizing principle. This is what we mean by the modern concept of race.

Insofar as race is popularly understood as a "social construction," this book argues that it is also learned as an "educational construction." It is not learned once and for all, but race is continually reinforced as a perspective on the world, a way to explain social and individual development. In the United States, it is difficult to understand national history without a central appreciation for race relations. Curriculum is part of this understanding as it organizes people's otherwise informal experience with race into a formal set of information, perspectives, and expectations. It teaches students how race matters (or does not matter) in their concrete lives.

For example, the curriculum can exclude students of color when it revolves around Eurocentric views, such as focusing primarily on the history and accomplishments of European societies and cultures, or relating history from the perspective of Europeans. By neglecting to include the history of non-Western peoples and places, the curriculum sends an implicit message to students of color that their own ancestors' accomplishments are not worthy of attention, that their accomplishments do not account for much. In the process, these students also learn that they are not significant, which compromises their education. Columbus's "discovery" of North America and its inhabitants has been analyzed for valorizing Europe's place in the world through its inventors and explorers, often obscuring the tremendous violence that Europeans visited upon indigenous populations.

When curriculum is tentative about the history of racism, it constructs differences in race power among groups as essentially peripheral, rather than central, to national development. And when curriculum fails to incorporate the perspectives of people of color, it adds to their marginalization in the academic sphere. The curriculum project becomes a racial project. Expressed another way, creating the curriculum entails describing the role that race groups play in history, which it may portray through Eurocentric biases that result in an incomplete and truncated history. This dynamic takes away from racial minority students' ability to excel when they do not see themselves reflected in the curriculum. On the other hand, it provides White students with a sense of entitlement and elevates their self-efficacy.

Multiculturalism and the Cultural Wars

The heyday of curriculum debates surrounding race occurred during the 1990s. Although historic debates between Booker T. Washington and W. E. B. Du Bois were vigorous earlier in the 20th century with respect to the economic independence of Black communities for the former and their political rights for the latter, and the Ethnic Studies Movement took hold in the 1970s, it was not until the 1990s that the United States witnessed what are now called the "cultural wars" within curriculum creation. Developments in "intercultural education" influenced this process, but multiculturalism and curricular change raged in the 1990s as a response to the entrenchment of a Eurocentric curriculum. The official canon of literature from Europe dominant in most public schools and universities, such as Shakespeare's plays and Dickens's novels, were put in direct conversation with Richard Wright's *Native Son* and Sandra Cisneros's *The House on Mango Street*. As one of the great upheavals involving race relations in schools, curriculum reform in the 1990s represented a shift in the official knowledge that students study—from the "Great Canon" to a "Multicultural Canon." Although this was certainly a product of the multicultural movement, it was also anti-racist and equity-minded in its intent and not only a call to respect diversity.

During this period, the United States experienced unprecedented public dialogue about the racial nature of the curriculum. The debate touched all levels of education, from K–12 to universities. From testing to teaching, race rose to the level of common sense and became part of national dialogue. Public schools considered new basal readers that included stories about and written by people of color, racially sensitive ways to teach science, and ethnomathematics, or conceiving of mathematics and science— previously thought to be free of culture—as now reflective of their social context. This perspective has its proponents as well as its detractors. With respect to science and mathematics, the point is not necessarily to question whether or not physical laws, like gravity, work the same way across cultures; of course they do. The goal is to situate their meaning within people's cultural understanding and the way science and mathematics may meet their survival and other needs. For instance, using mathematics to erect tall office buildings in Los Angeles carries different meanings and addresses different needs from using mathematics to solve the hunger problem in some African nations or making affordable housing accessible in Mexico. During this time, state history frameworks were also targeted and revisionist history became the alternative to official History. In higher education, the University of California, Berkeley instituted an "American Cultures" requirement that undergraduate students must fulfill when they finished courses on racial and ethnic diversity. Multiculturalism became a household term with diversity and equity its mantra.

On one side, arguments for the "best" that society has produced seek to protect the Western-based canon. Fearing the dilution of excellence by a movement characterized as appeasing vocal racial minorities, defenders of the official canon justify the existing curriculum as tried and true knowledge. As the argument goes, Western knowledge is the basis of U.S. schooling because it represents a superior form and needs no apology. It is not a racialized perspective, but a set of facts that unveil the true nature of history, science, and culture. Western knowledge apprehends the true order of things as they exist in their natural state. It is not a special interest group furthering its own agenda, unlike multiculturalists, anti-racists, and ethnocentric educators, whose concern is self-esteem rather than truth.

Multiculturalists are characterized as a special interest group that prioritizes fighting for its rights and raising minority students' self-awareness over the importance of accurately understanding history and other subject areas. For example, Arthur Schlesinger, Jr. (1998) cited multiple factually incorrect instances in Afrocentric history, a movement that became popular in the late 1980s to early 1990s; he claimed it made a mockery of the discipline of History. To Allan Bloom (1987), the opening of the American curriculum led to the "closing of the American mind" and the slippery slide toward mediocrity of its universities. The timeless work of Shakespeare and other canonized literature are diminished in exchange for ethnocentric demands for change. The victim here is an education worth the name, whose rigor is sacrificed for the sake of politics, specifically racial equality, which produces its own set of problems.

The stakes are obvious. A curriculum that features little in the way of minority representation damages the self-image and worth of minority students. But multiculturalizing the curriculum arguably also enriches the students of the dominant culture by broadening their appreciation for history and the arts. It is not forged simply in the interests of students of color, but provides White students with the opportunity to conceive of their history and experience as part of a larger social process. James Banks (2005) has recast multiculturalism as a national curriculum in a country where racial diversity is the norm. In other words, a multicultural curriculum is precisely representative of the national culture defined by group differences, not a form of special interest. In this light, Eurocentrists emerge as the special interest group because they argue for something other than the existing diversity in the nation, but instead a specific slice of it.

In fact, a Eurocentric curriculum is arguably inaccurate because its objectivity is compromised if the social and historical development of society is limited to a partial perspective. This is what Sandra Harding (1991) referred to when she considered that science, for example, under the dominant control of men becomes a form of "weak objectivity." Instead, strong objectivity takes into consideration the participation and contribution of women to the scientific endeavor either through their own scientific work or the labor they provide so that male scientists may go about their work. Similarly, we can say that a multicultural curriculum enables educators and students to appreciate a more expansive "truth," insofar as it captures a larger swathe of it. This does not suggest that the minority perspective is right by virtue of its marginalized status. Multiculturalists do not suggest that racial minorities necessarily possess the accurate understanding of social processes. Multiculturalism does not diminish European accomplishments, but puts them in a conversation with world development.

Multiculturalism is not meant for minority students as such, but for a national populace formed as much out of difference as it is out of sameness. It affirms the American mantra of "*E pluribus unum*," or "in the one the many." It addresses the long-standing racial imbalance in the curriculum, which has favored the accomplishments of Europeans. Challenging this dominant tradition does not diminish the advances made by Europe, but enlarges students' sense of world civilizations, appreciation for difference, and notions of citizenship. Eurocentrists worry about Balkanization as a possible outcome of diversifying the curriculum, which is not unfounded. They may even suggest that reducing Western perspectives to a singular is inaccurate because a multiplicity of perspectives hails from Europe (of course, multiculturalists may level the same objection, emphasizing the heterogeneity of minority perspectives). A national curriculum that represents one perspective over others is already limited, if not also provincial. Putting its best foot forward, multicultural curriculum is a form of cosmopolitanism, or a certain intellectual worldliness that appreciates difference and an expanded notion of community. By definition, it is not ethnocentric because it encourages multi-perspectives on educational topics (hence the "multi" in multiculturalism).

The input of people of color representing various interests (e.g., scholars, educators, and parents) is also a consideration so that their voice is validated, not to mention creating a more democratic procedure for curriculum formation. We do not want to romanticize equitable participation and the challenges to forging an educational process for it. In fact, the general theme of civic participation remains outside the scope of this book, but we acknowledge that civic participation in education is part of the democratic process. In fact, James Banks (2006) considered the democratic transformation of school culture to be one of the last stages of multicultural reform. With respect to ameliorating racism, the means (democratic process) to the end product (multicultural curriculum) is also important.

Public deliberation, even debate, on curriculum formation speaks to the issue of racism because it asks central questions about the constitution of the public sphere and its institutions like schools. Because people of color do not gain entry into positions of power—from the academy, to communities, and to governance—with nearly the frequency of White Americans, including perspectives of color in curriculum decisions means wrestling with the issue of increasing their presence. Short of their full inclusion, it is necessary to speak for them in their absence. In all, the suggestion is that communities of color could be included more robustly, indeed welcomed, as equal partners in the forging of the curriculum. They can share in all its victories as well as its failures, rather than be reduced to spectators on the academic sidelines or relegated to the back of the intellectual bus.

Race and Knowledge

As already mentioned, if people of color are not represented in the overt curriculum, it is difficult to enter more nuanced arguments about its nature. Indeed, including them in the curriculum is already a Herculean task. Fortunately, multiculturalism has made significant progress in this regard. Once minorities are represented more equally with Whites, educators consider other issues that are equally important. Curriculum's etymology is "race course," which implies a certain connection that it maintains with notions of competition. At least implicit in this root meaning is curriculum as a game. But it begs the question, "What game is being played?" Additionally, "What are the rules and who makes them?"

If we play with the etymology of curriculum for the purposes of this book, then the course is about "race." The competition is centered on knowing a set of materials, even mastery of it. In the past, curriculum comprised a set of racialized information, passing itself off as universal knowledge. On a deeper level, it is a racialized knowledge system, which is precisely about what sets of worthy questions are posed by the curriculum and how they are answered in turn. It brings up the fact that certain questions may not enter the conversation. In this section, we discuss curriculum as a relation of power, and suggest that this power is enacted through knowledge as a way of representing the known world. It speaks to a second (by no means secondary) level of representation, which is how people are understood and made intelligible through textbooks and other school material. Now that people of color are included in the official curriculum more frequently, *how* are they described and written about?

The way that people are written into textbooks, how they are included in stories about history, and constructed as characters in novels and artistic work, influence our understanding of them. Omission from the official curriculum is not the only way that racism in education is enacted. How people of color are portrayed through knowledge may also do the work of racism. If curriculum serves as a reflection of society, what kind of image stares back at the student?

Knowledge is not an inert thing, but a dynamic relation into which educators enter. Knowledge is not set once and for all, independent of context and history. It is not waiting to be discovered and all educators have to do is find an appropriate language to express it. Unlike gravity, social knowledge, like race, entails a good dose of invention. This does not suggest that school knowledge is plainly made up. For it to make sense, it touches and tells someone's reality. This does not mean that it is unreliable, but neither does it suggest that knowledge production is a purely scientific process absent of political interest. Once established, forms of knowledge, even false ones, do a great deal of work.

Knowledge is a human creation forged in order to achieve particular ends. By and large, knowledge is the business of schools; they teach it, test it, and encourage its mastery. But knowledge is also a way to tell a story, of framing an otherwise disconnected set of facts and events. Knowledge connects them and provides order to the social world. In particular, race knowledge frames the story as much as a piece of art is contained within a picture frame to set it off from its surrounding wall or room. Framing the curriculum regulates how race history unfolds by giving it shape, providing its sequence of events, and stamping it with a sense of time.

In these important ways, knowledge and its institutionalization through the curriculum become the story of race, the point being that it could have been built with another plan in place, a different story to tell. The ability to make race history known in a particular manner is a form of power because it encourages certain questions to be asked and discourages others. Although this power is never closed off and makes possible alternative accounts of race history, shifting the official curriculum is never easy and its official form is invested with institutional power. Seen this way, knowledge is not just an idea in the head, but a resource around which people in power build institutions like schools. As we see with Eurocentrism, this knowledge is guarded and protected.

Today, race has become common sense, a way of knowing society and explaining its evolution. In Western societies, like the United States, it is difficult to comprehend, even analyze, social processes without accounting for race. More important, race is a way of knowing ourselves as social beings. It defines our identity in fundamental ways and the curriculum may reinforce the status quo or challenge it. Conceived this way, curriculum decisions around race are not only a bookish concern with knowledge, but are about the kind of society people desire.

"Knowledge is power" is a well-known saying popularized at the height of the Civil Rights Movement. Its other variation is "Speaking truth to power." These simple phrases suggest that knowing accurately the processes responsible for the current racial predicament is liberating. Knowing the history of racial power is then understood as a form of empowerment. For people of color, a curriculum that unveils the inner workings of racism confirms their experience with racism and validates their worldview, this time sanctioned by the official curriculum and given its proper weight. For Whites, it means something quite different; mainly, but not always, it comes with a sense of complicity accompanied by difficult emotions such as guilt and shame. But like people of color, Whites may also walk away with a sense of clarity about a state of affairs that intimately affects their lives.

A new curriculum may not change schools and society, but no social change happens without it, either before or after major upheavals. It may happen before, as a way of preparing for or inciting change. It may happen after, as a logical outcome of sweeping social transformations. Of course, change is not always progressive and former president Ronald Reagan's conservative platform is one example of rolling back certain protections for which race-conscious educators fought. To the extent that these kinds of reform intensify rather than change racial power, they reinforce knowledge in the interest of existing relations and protect the people who benefit from them. They contribute to knowledge in the service of power.

However, as this section suggests, there is another way of looking at the relationship between knowledge and power. Rather than "knowledge is power," the simple inversion that "power is knowledge" argues that the ability to control knowledge about people is a way to control them. What does this mean? Controlling knowledge is a way to define how a racial group and its history are understood. Because people act based on the knowledge they presume about others, curricular knowledge produces racial actions. If students are encouraged to believe in history as based on uncontroversial sets of facts, they conceive of racial events as essentially fixed and given. Therefore, understanding history as a process or perspective becomes an exercise in futility because history could not have worked out otherwise or be interpreted differently.

This is racial curriculum as a form of transmitted knowledge. The tension in history, its interpretation, and the struggle over its representation are political processes separated from the official curriculum. It does not appreciate the creative dimension of curriculum making filtered through the racial imagination of its makers. Because schooling is often characterized as the process whereby knowledge is transmitted from teacher to student, students are led down the path of accepting the images and histories presented to them. Teaching and learning become a matter of how to master the information presented to students, rather than teaching them to think critically about it. Racial power is relegated to areas of life considered extracurricular, such as housing and the division of labor, rather than something happening in the interaction between students and the pages of their books.

Curricular knowledge setting is a selective process of highlighting events in history, giving them special meaning, and positioning racial groups within their retelling. In the past, when Black students learned that they appear in two specific periods of history—namely, slavery and the Civil Rights Movement—curricular knowledge constructs them as relatively absent from the rest of U.S. development. This characterization has improved over the decades, but points out the basic importance of curricular framing. In this sense, the curriculum sets the parameters for the known world, spatially and temporally. With respect to time, recognizing the continuity that connects the long stretches between enslavement and the Civil Rights Movement means that the second's arrival owes something to the first; indeed, the latter may have been historically determined by the former. In other words, Black people's early slave status later gives way to their second-class citizen status, requiring the momentous Civil Rights Acts to follow.

If discussions around curriculum do not account for the spatial orientation of history, then it narrates U.S. development from an unquestioned place of beginning. That is, starting with slavery is a southern as well as a northeastern story, which then illuminates the nation's racial strife from a certain vantage point. That is, it begins from a geographical origin and therefore defines the terrain, actors, and plot. It frames educators' explanations and influences their understanding of racial history. If slavery is where the story begins, then the narrative is implicitly framed within a Black–White understanding.

However, this plot line looks very different if considered from a southwestern sensibility, where contestation over land ownership is arguably the dominant narrative between Anglos and Mexicans, and Native Americans and White settlers. Race as territory, rather than race as skin color, becomes the defining unit of analysis and shifts the knowledge necessary to explain this dynamic. It does not mean that race as skin color is absent in the discourse of race as territory. This important fact notwithstanding, it speaks to a struggle within the curriculum over representation of racial matters and its defining moments. A southern–northeastern narrative may stress the Emancipation Proclamation of 1863, whereas a southwestern-inspired framework may emphasize the Treaty of Guadalupe Hidalgo of 1848 between the United States and Mexico where the latter ceded huge chunks of land to the former. A curriculum's ordering of knowledge comes with racial consequences.

Ultimately, a curriculum that attests to these complexities arrives at a fuller picture of racism, which is the goal. The argument is less about whether the southern–northeastern or southwestern perspective is more appropriate, but how race struggle is defined differently in each case. In fact, it is possible that pitting one minority group's experience with racism against another leads to Balkanization or a fragmented grasp of racial power, so educators may want to guard against this possibility. In addition, emphasizing history at the margins does not promote neglecting the center, in this case, Whites. After all, racism in either case incorporates minority groups into the racial predicament *in relation to Whiteness*, or the ideology that upholds White superiority.

A curriculum that demystifies racism presents multiple vantage points from groups who have been affected by it. These nuances do not detract from a clearer understanding of racial domination, but arguably put it in better focus. For the complexity of the racial picture requires an equally complex set of lenses in order to apprehend it. Knowledge of race relations is always an issue of "knowledge for what purpose?"

In James Banks's (2006) model of multicultural school reform, one of the founders of this school of thought adds "cultural transformation" as the final stage and goal of curriculum change. In other words, not satisfied with a definition of knowledge as something in the head, he places it squarely into our hands as a way to transform nature into culture, and to transform culture into a new society. Thus, knowledge is not an inert thing, but may be used to accomplish certain ends. A curriculum that mystifies racial history, oversimplifies it, or considers it knowledge that is objective and uncontroversial, does students of any race a disservice.

Curricular Knowledge and the Knower

Another way in which curriculum becomes a way to regulate knowledge is through its ability to define not only the known world, but who exists as knowers in that world. As presumed knowers, Whites or Euro-Americans occupy the center of knowledge, whereas minorities exist at its margins. Minorities have been subject to the controlling system of Western knowledge since at least the Enlightenment, or that era of European development marked by scientific progress on the one hand and the classification of the species on the other, including humans. In this schema, Europeans, particularly their Western and Northern varieties, represent the highest form of development. As part of the racial organization of society and the racial order that arises from it, knowledge from the knower is deemed legitimate, whereas information from the objects of knowledge is suspect.

We could reduce this conversation to knowledge's proximity to science, but this would oversimplify the expansive reach of race relations. Knowledge born from art and literature, politics and philosophy, attest to the existence of Europe's way of life and the relative insignificance of non-Western societies. Although multiculturalism has made progress in questioning this problematic history in curriculum formation, the tendency to construct Westerners as ultimate knowers is an orientation that has no real challenger as far as schools are concerned. From the indigenous knowledge of North and South America, to African cultures, to Asian systems of thought, U.S. schools have not fully incorporated non-Western knowledge into their thought process. Students are introduced to them, but it is difficult to discern if they influence how students actually think about the world around them. They are exposed to non-Western cultures, which is different from being fundamentally changed by them.

Charles Mills (1997) has called this process the "racial contract." At once an abstract contract (i.e., not a "real" contract) that Whites created to divide the social world into humans (read: Europeans) and sub-humans (read: people of color), the racial ramifications of the contract also include creating group relations with respect to knowledge. The educational version of the racial contract is the attempt to distinguish knowers from sub-knowers, whereby the first group is identified with White students and the second with minorities. In the history of contact between the West and the rest, the relationship is most overt in the curriculum with respect to the Age of Discovery, wherein Europeans claim to "discover" non-European lands and their peoples. Fortunately, this assumption has now been problematized in many educational circles, including educational materials by the collective Rethinking Schools, reconsidering Columbus's history. Not fully able to resolve the issue, however, the general revision has tended to reframe European explorers as having discovered places like the Americas *for* Europe. Unfortunately, the implicit message is that it took Europeans to generate knowledge about these places, to bring them into official existence.

As scientific classifications about the natural world emerged in Europe, they were applied problematically to the social world of humans. Just as a hierarchy exists in the animal kingdom, it was argued that the darker parts of the world produced ways of knowing that are inherently inferior to Western knowledge. As a result, it takes an enlightened eye to study non-Western societies and generate knowledge about them, to know them better than they know themselves, indeed to make them known to themselves. Because Africans and indigenous populations are assumed to speak less developed languages and practice less advanced traditions, they must be spoken for or represented. When re-education to learn the Western curriculum, such as boarding schools for Native Americans in the U.S. context, is not possible, education is withheld completely, as was the case with African Americans during slavery. In another instance, a curriculum in a language entirely incomprehensible to Asian American students sparked the move toward bilingual education in the landmark case of *Lau v. Nichols*. The racial contract is arguably still in place in order to differentiate the world into knowers and objects of knowledge. Its version in schools may be labeled the "educational racial contract."

Edward Said's study of "Orientalism" (1979) confirmed the racial implications of knowledge relations when one group occupies the status of knower over another. In his study of the relations between the Occident (Europe) and the Orient (the Middle East), Said documented modern forms of imperialism. For example, when Napoleon waged war against Egypt, the emperor did not only bring soldiers and guns; he brought with him an arsenal of intellectuals and scholars. Where military domination fell short, Napoleon would exercise control over Egypt through the route of knowledge and culture. Upon their return to France, Napoleon and his "army" brought with them reams and reams of documents that surveyed the Orient's natural and social world. Confirming historical instances when the pen is mightier than the sword, these collections speak volumes of France's ability to assert itself as a nation of knowers, putting the French in a position of advantage over the "Orientals."

The consequences of Orientalism are far-reaching and instructive for an understanding of the curriculum as a knowledge relation. Orientalism created a knowledge industry (sometimes touring) about the Orient, and defined how it should be written into history and therefore into existence. Not only did it enable the Occident to control how Orientals ultimately would be understood, it also projected how Europeans understood themselves in the process. Therefore, knowledge of the East serves the West in terms of dominating non-Westerners through ideological images, stereo-typical descriptions, and cultural oversimplifications. As this knowledge industry is consumed by other Westerners, their interactions with non-Westerners become politically laden, filled with projections of what "ideal" Orientals are like. Often such interactions are presupposed, sometimes replaced, by indirect experiences with the Other that Europeans read about in the literature or confront through the arts.

Like a curriculum, information about the Orient substitutes for actual interactions between Westerners and Orientals. As a result, understanding the concrete lives of the Other is exchanged for texts about them; Orientals themselves become textbooks to be read and consumed. When face-to-face interactions do occur, they are filtered through the impressions gained from brochures and leaflets about the Orient, which are never innocent. Sometimes these dominant representations are internalized by the colonized or subordinate races.

Said's findings (1979) provide an appropriate analogy regarding the racial nature of the curriculum. For example, in the scholarship on Black families, particularly those in urban settings, for many decades before the 1980s, there is a veritable monopoly by White intellectuals regarding their representation. With the arrival of William Julius Wilson's work (1978), this industry opened up to Black or non-White intellectuals. In any decade leading up to that point, White scholars dominated the research centered on portrayals of Black culture, usually a pathologized image of it, or what has been called the "culture of poverty." We note that the academy was itself White-dominated, but call attention to the capacity of research knowledge to outlast its authors, long after the field has opened up to minorities.

In Glazer and Moynihan's (1970) report, the pattern we note is a consistent portrait of Black families as lacking necessary resources to succeed in schools. We discuss some of this dynamic through Bourdieu's concept of "cultural capital" in Chapter 3. From culture to nurture, Black families fall short. Summed up in the phrase "culture of poverty," Black life is described as developing cultural practices that function as responses to ghettoization, lacking employment opportunities, and experiencing other forms of social isolation. Extending what Said (1979) found in Orientalism, we suggest that this literature supports Whites as knowers and Blacks as objects of that knowledge. Often, Whites' depictions of Black communities emphasize the latter's inadequacies rather than the former's culpability.

Racism in the curriculum is directly implicated by this set of representations. First, a wave of policies directly resulting from the "Black problem" crested over the United States. From the war on poverty to the war on drugs to the current war on schools, minority children became the problem that must be fixed. This tendency did not go unchallenged as the 1970s also witnessed counter-representations of Black coping strategies as creative or generative, and not merely self-defeating. But these valiant attempts notwithstanding, education is still haunted by the damaging images of minority life produced by culture of poverty narratives. The curriculum does not escape as it becomes the symbol of the knowledge base that students of color are assumed to need in order to succeed. But like the previous century's Orientalism, the curriculum produces one-dimensional accounts of minority children, from the failures of Blacks and Latinos to the successes of Asian Americans who are model students on the one hand, but perpetual foreigners on the other.

Concluding this chapter on curriculum formation and its participation in race relations, we suggest that in addition to the curriculum as a technical text, a document of educational goals and outcomes, and an assessment tool to determine the learning that has taken place, it is also an introduction to a way of life. This means that the curriculum is also central to producing that life, and in the case of the United States, it involves coming to terms with the history and upkeep of race. It could be argued that the curriculum is many things, but we suggest that it is a knowledge relation that educators use, which helps to construct the racial world. In other words, the curriculum performs a certain work and from this purpose certain outcomes are produced.

When it fails to account for race, by default, if not by design, the curriculum reinforces current racial arrangements. But created deliberately to ameliorate this predicament, the curriculum may also challenge racism and in doing so serves other ends that educators may nurture and advance. Multiculturalism enters its second generation, a way paved by its creators in the figures of James Banks and others. By and large, this cohort of scholars succeeded in shifting schools from being defenders of Eurocentrism to adopting diversity as the new common sense. It was no small feat and new battles are being waged, such as *how much* or *what kind* of diversity to incorporate. Even those who emphasize the canon of "dead White men" do so within the language of multiculturalism by arguing that they are part of American diversity. Curriculum reform is by no means the panacea and there are other nodes in the education system that need to be addressed. One of those areas is culturally relevant education, which while certainly connected to curricular matters, is another issue altogether. This is where we turn in the next chapter.

Study Questions

1. At specific grade levels, how much of the curriculum material is devoted to the issue of race or its problems of racism and racial discrimination?

2. What proportion of the curriculum accounts for material dedicated to racial minorities, or people of color?

3. Under what context do people of color appear in the curriculum? Are they central or peripheral?

4. What images are associated with people of color and Whites in the curriculum? In other words, how are they represented?

5. As far as you can decipher, are there instances where people of color represent themselves or are they consistently represented for?

6. Are minority representations oversimplified or complex?

7. Does the curriculum frame minorities as problem solvers or as problems to be solved?

Selected Readings

Apple, M. (2004). *Ideology and curriculum.* 3rd Ed. New York: RoutledgeFalmer.

Banks, J. (2005). Multicultural education: Characteristics and goals. In J. Banks & C. Banks (Eds.), *Multicultural education: Issues and perspectives* (pp. 3–30). 5th Ed. New York: Wiley.

Banks, J. (2006). *Race, culture, and education.* New York: Routledge.

Bloom, A. (1987). *The closing of the American mind.* New York: Simon & Schuster Inc.

Buras, K. (2008). *Rightist multiculturalism.* New York: Routledge.

Du Bois, W. E. B. (1989). *The souls of black folk.* New York: Penguin Books. First published in 1904.

Glazer, N. & Moynihan, P. (1970). *Beyond the melting pot.* 2nd Ed. Cambridge, MA: The MIT Press.

Harding, S. (1991). *Whose science? Whose knowledge?,* Ithaca, NY: Cornell University Press.

Kliebard, H. (1995). *The struggle for the American curriculum 1893–1958.* 2nd Ed. New York: Routledge & Kegan Paul.

Mills, C. (1997). *The racial contract.* Ithaca, NY: Cornell University Press.

Said, E. (1979). *Orientalism.* New York: Random House.

Schlesinger, J. (1998). *The disuniting of America: Reflections on a multicultural society.* 2nd Ed. New York: W.W. Norton & Company.

Swartz, E. (1992). Emancipatory narratives: Rewriting the master script in the school curriculum. *Journal of Negro Education, 61*(3), 341–355.

Wilson, W. J. (1978). *The declining significance of race.* Chicago, IL: University of Chicago Press.

Culturally Relevant Education and Racism

Education for Relevance

The Black students walk into the classroom and after milling around for a minute, take their seats. Their teacher, who shares their cultural orientation, heads to her desk and after setting her materials down, she calls for their attention. The students keep talking and catching up on their weekend exploits and the woman uses her teacher voice to repeat herself. The students perk up and take notice. Some even look fearful, not in the way that one fears someone else's mother, but rather one's own. The teacher looks down at her teaching schedule as the students wait, some of them whispering to each other. The teacher looks up and surveys the room. The whispering students halt in their speech.

As the teacher begins today's lessons, she uses a linguistic style that is compatible with the students' own way of relating, familiar to their cultural repertoire. She uses social references that they understand, which are relevant for their learning development as they assimilate new information into pre-existing schemata. Not only does she use linguistic practices that resonate with the children's home background, she also uses gestures that tap into their collective meaning systems. In other words, from language, to gestures, to classroom material, the teacher uses a pedagogy that is relevant to the students, which, while no protection from mediocre student performance, or even failure, is assumed to be a basic ingredient to effective teaching. Certainly not signaling the end product, it begins the process.

Of course, it is easier to imagine the scene above in the context of Jim Crow schooling in the United States, a form of legalized inferior education for Blacks when Black teachers taught Black students and a cultural match was arguably in place. There was cultural relevance in the classroom, a social match between the young learner and the adult in the figure of the teacher. But it would be difficult to romanticize this situation, taking place as it did in the limiting context of *de jure*, or legalized, segregation. Even though the learning interaction was culturally relevant, it occurred in a coerced condition where Black students could not attend the same schools as Whites, confirmed by the *Plessy v. Ferguson* ruling that separate schools could be equal.

Despite the cultural similarities between students and teachers, particularly for Black communities, relevant education within legalized segregation had a ceiling to contend with, such as Blacks' second-class status in the broader sphere of education and division of labor. In addition, cultural relevance should not compete with having up-to-date books and other basic educational materials, wholly lacking in Jim Crow schools. Later in 1954, this arrangement would be struck down by the *Brown v. Board of Education, Topeka* ruling, which deemed separate schooling as inherently unequal.

As the United States decided that integration was the higher good, a new era of desegregation efforts began in earnest, culminating in the Civil Rights Act of 1968. With respect to schools, the era of *Plessy* gave way to the *Brown* era and education entered the challenge of integrating schools. There were many solutions put forth, including busing children from their neighborhood schools in an effort to integrate schools more broadly; this is now generally acknowledged to have failed, among the reasons being that the responsibility of busing rested on the shoulders of Black families, a burden that was never equally shared by White families. In addition, it did not address the racial climate of integrated schools. An outcome was that in contrast to Jim Crow schools, more Black students now had a White woman as their teacher. This meant that the cultural match that Black students previously experienced during Jim Crow gave way to the challenge of cultural mismatch between Black or minority children and White adults in the classroom. For our analysis, it brings up the observation that solutions often come with new sets of problems, a recurring theme in these chapters. The challenge of White teachers overseeing the development of Black and other children of color proved daunting. Whereas during legal segregation, Black students could rely on cultural sympathy from their teachers, White educators were now teaching "other people's children."

Although few educators would desire to roll back Civil Rights to the time before *Brown*, they also face the cultural crevasse between learners and teachers as a logical outcome of integration. There have been countless attempts to sensitize a predominantly White teaching force with information, training, and personal and professional experiences in order to bridge the gap. Thus, despite the noble attempt to desegregate schools, educators now provided Black students with a culturally non-relevant education. Something incredible was gained with integration, but admittedly something was lost.

The *Brown* decision addressed the social or legal form of racial segregation, but came up short in approaching the cultural divide among the races, which is difficult to mandate with the required "deliberate speed" of the Civil Rights Acts. Whereas with Jim Crow, Blacks were sent to the back of the academic bus, post-*Brown* education was like a bus where people may lawfully integrate, but are at a loss regarding how they might interact. The overt racism of the first was replaced by the well-intentioned but incomplete solutions of the second. Education in the United States was challenged by the uncomfortable realization that schooling remained largely non-relevant to the cultural worldview of many students of color. It seemed that the bus had become resegregated.

As with any chapter in this book, we do not suggest that any change, even radical, in one aspect of education could sufficiently challenge racism. As the tale above makes clear, culturally relevant education for students of color, which is defined as one that resonates with and is sympathetic to their meaning systems, by itself is not enough, especially if it happens within broader conditions of racial inequality. It is readily apparent that culturally sensitive education within Jim Crow arrangements is a form of relevant schooling, but within conditions that are not sustainable. All this said, it would be problematic to suggest that culturally relevant education has to happen in a context where the teacher and students share the same racial identity. This is neither practical in an increasingly diverse nation, nor necessarily a preferred method within the perspective of multiculturalism or anti-racism. We recognize that ethnocentric charter schools and Historically Black Colleges and Universities (HBCUs) produce conditions that raise the self-esteem, levels of participation, and in the end, overall success of students of color. In the higher good of an integrated society and school system, however, there would be no need for them as diverse racial groups found a sense of belonging in the common school experience. Although this is admittedly a condition currently not in place, this book anticipates its coming, not as a matter of inevitability, but as a preferable state of affairs.

Cultural relevance is not a panacea, for it does not explain the success of certain segments of African American and Latino students. Admittedly, these students come largely from middle-class homes, but it suffices to suggest that their cultural background or racial upbringing is at least part of their success, which avoids a deficit model that frames their culture as only leading to failure. The rising status of Asian American students, for whom an American education is largely culturally non-relevant, is harder to explain, if we go by the measure that a Eurocentric curriculum or White-dominated teaching force do not represent a good match with Asian American culture. They seem to do well *despite* the cultural non-relevance of their education. Yet, the Asian American case is not this straightforward.

In education, with some exceptions and geographical specificities, Asian American students have become associated with educational achievement. Their mathematical proficiency and stories about their possession of the "math gene" are sometimes heard. This stereotype may readily be dispelled if we remember that because they face linguistic discrimination, Asian American students who speak languages other than English may gravitate toward mathematics and science as alternative avenues to success. In other words, their relative success in mathematics and science may have more to do with their investment in those fields rather than natural inclinations toward them. It has little to do with their racial identity as such and more with their racial positioning in society and their responses to it. Facing linguistic discrimination, they concentrate their energy on mathematics and science.

It is tempting to explain Asian American achievement by arguing that they are smarter, their families have good values, or that they prioritize education. Often, the subtext is, "Why can't Black or Latino families be more like them?" Such arguments about Asian American "model minority status" are used to discipline other minority groups. They are used as examples to dispel the notion that racism limits minorities. If a group of color could succeed in the United States, it is *prima facie* evidence that other minorities could succeed. Just as often, Asian Americans become buffers wedged between the Black–White anxiety: too much of color for Whites, too close to White for Blacks. They feel the pressure to side with one experience, Black or White, even though neither one represents their position.

This is illustrated by a scene from Spike Lee's movie, *Do the Right Thing*, when an Asian grocer faces possible violence during an urban riot. He screams, "Me Black, me not White, me Black." Although he has interest in self-preservation and wants to avoid violence, the grocer's response is symptomatic of Asian American racial positioning in the United States as a buffer group. It seems at least plausible that Asian American educational ascendance is a response to blocked opportunities in politics, entertainment, and other avenues for social mobility. Education is their road to social mobility.

Although we may be able to speak of honorable mentions—such as film director Ang Lee, journalist Lisa Ling, and basketball player Jeremy Linn in entertainment and sports; and former secretary of transportation Norman Mineta and Associate Justice Goodwin Liu in politics—Asian Americans have generally lacked access to these spheres. Even a cursory look at public life bears out the utter lack of Asian American public figures and self-generated images. Experiencing structural limitations on these fronts, they have built cultural understandings that favor education as their road to success. Without education, Asian American prospects look pretty limited. Thus, their educational predicament is probably due to race as a social condition.

It is also possible to argue that schooling is experienced by most young people as lacking relevance to their daily lives, including White students. That is, if we believe that the child developmentalists of the early 20th century were correct in their appraisal of formal education as out of sync with children's "natural" inclinations (however they are defined, especially in the current focus on standardization), then all children, regardless of race, are victims of a non-relevant education. If this is correct, by definition, schooling for externally driven outcomes is more a process of socialization for prescribed ends than it is an education to cultivate an individual's talents. Here we use socialization conceptually to mean a form of social control, not the more acceptable sense of socialization as the induction of children into the broader cultural milieu; in contrast to this, education is a way to realize human potential. It is safe to say that, even for White students, basketball player and rapper Shaquille O'Neal of the 1990s is more relevant than Shakespeare of the 1590s. If this portrayal is compelling, then there is reason to question modern education's relevance for most children, not just for minority students. As many studies of youth culture suggest, schooling is out of sync with their priorities and preferences. Most children would be likely to prefer playing over reading a book or manipulating a mathematics equation.

Be that as it may, it is logical that if education were more culturally relevant to minority students, particularly Blacks and Latinos who struggle, this would go some distance toward raising their achievement. Culturally relevant education, or its other family of terms—e.g., responsive, sensitive, or contextualized—does not argue that families of color do not bear responsibilities for accommodating official school culture; many have tried. Instead, it investigates the school's culture for its inability to tap into the resources that non-mainstream children bring to it, which often go unnoticed. For children of color, a culturally non-relevant education represents another layer of injury that White students do not experience. Of course, it comes with no guarantees, but like the Chinese students in San Francisco in the *Lau v. Nichols* case, for whom an education in English made little sense, minority students learning within a cultural context that is strange to their worldview do not take long to realize that schools do not value their culture. Whether or not culturally relevant education could ultimately transform the school system for minority students is a larger, historical question.

With respect to minority students with high attainment, such as Asian Americans, it stands to reason that they would achieve even more highly if their education were a better match with their cultural background. Asian American achievement is not an argument against culturally relevant education, as if a speedboat could not go faster if it were provided with a bigger engine. It would be tempting to argue that for Asian Americans, educational discipline would be consistent with their cultural worldview. But as we mentioned above, their intense orientation toward education is probably a response to their own understandings of their chances for social mobility. For White students, who still must travel the educational gap between their preferred youth culture and school culture, the distance is arguably shorter and the terrain more familiar.

Although it would be accurate to claim that in general Shakespeare has had less influence on White students than Shaquille, *Beowulf* less than the Back Street Boys, there are "echoes" of European culture in school that resonate with them. Put this together with teaching styles that more closely resemble their cultural cognitive processes, communication patterns that are congruent with their family habits, and a pattern emerges that puts White students at an advantage. The point is that no single cultural practice could accomplish this edge for White students, but *schooling as an entire experience taken into consideration* adds up and produces predictable results.

White students experience a racial lift by virtue of not having necessarily to negotiate a culture in schools that is foreign to them. Racially speaking, they have experienced a culturally relevant education for many decades; educators are now beginning to insist on the same consideration for students of color. White children may have many struggles, including class differences, but cultural mismatch via race in school is not one of them. They may still receive a non-relevant education because of contextual reasons that prevent them from thriving, but *they* are not irrelevant to their own education. Their cultural understanding forms part of their education and is not external to it.

The Two Sides of Culture: Universals and Particulars

If high test scores are the assumed goal of education in the climate of standardization, particularly since the enactment of No Child Left Behind, then culture is arguably what makes education meaningful. We will have more to say about standardizing education in Chapter 6. Our invocation of culture in this chapter is informed by an understanding that it is a set of practices that makes an otherwise disconnected social existence meaningful, that it represents a fundamental part of human development, and that it is ultimately educative when cultivated. Defining culture in this manner includes the common sense version of it as practices "belonging" to or "owned" by a group, reductive as this view may be, but our attempt is to enlarge the discussion of culture to include the domain of meaning making.

As a daily practice, culture transforms human nature into specific sets of understanding for a group's survival. In this sense, culture is inherently specific because it is tied to a specified place and time for its creation. The Asian American emphasis on schooling mentioned above is one such instance, a cultural practice born out of a response to their social condition. Another instance may suffice. Although "jumping the broom" was an African practice by origin, during U.S. slavery, slaves used it in secrecy to signal the marriage between two people so as to go undetected by their White masters. Its meaning in an American context diverges from its

African significance because of the specific conditions during slavery, yet it maintains its special relationship to marriage within an African cultural mindset. Today, jumping the broom is still used in modern weddings all over the United States.

In the past, Euro-American culture was understood as a set of meanings that transcended its specific European context and condition. It was claimed as escaping its particularity as a form of understanding and graduating to the status of universality, something applicable to any human being. This position has become harder, if not impossible, to maintain with the advent of multiculturalism and a critique of Eurocentrism.

Educators are able to appreciate the ability of specific cultures to transcend their own conditioning, but Eurocentrism's claim to universality violates this sentiment when it becomes a synonym for a general human experience untainted by perspective, place, or predicament. On the other hand, when Western culture has been acknowledged as having particular origins and therefore is framed as culturally specific, it is promoted as superior to other cultures. This form of ethnocentrism, which is an element of racism, overestimates the accomplishments of European culture and underestimates those of other cultures in one related motion: the first as more than it is, the second as less than they are.

This does not mean that minority cultures do not come with their own set of problems and limitations, preventing cultural relativism from creeping into the picture. They are not different from Western culture in this regard. Their culture also speaks to aspects of what it means to be part of the general human species. As part of a dialectic, or a logic of both/ands rather than either/ors, culture bears the traits of universal humanity *and* the contextual particulars that all cultural groups experience. The pitfalls of depicting Euro-American culture as either universal and therefore race-neutral, or specific and consequently race-superior, lead to the same outcome of Whites' presumed racial superiority.

For much of U.S. education's history, Euro-American culture has been the unquestioned basis of education. In the past, this knowledge selection and learning process was transparent and needed little justification. It went without saying. With the rise of multiculturalism, Western centrality was challenged, compromised, and eventually reformed. Its cultural commitments became the subject of public discussions in education. Among these commitments was the premium put on the human capacity to reason, a distinguishing aspect of the species to Enlightenment thinkers. In U.S. schools, this tradition was the educational capacity to train the will through discipline, a now outmoded school of thought. It was not portrayed as a cultural habit *per se*, but as the mark of being human.

The goal of cultivating reason in students came with the promotion of certain dispositions, such as detachment, mental discipline, and the ultimate goal of autonomous rationality: that is, to think and judge ideas independently. Many of these characteristics continue today, found in Kohlberg's (1999) stages of moral reasoning and the Bloom (1999) taxonomy of educational objectives. These are formative findings in education, but at least in the case of Kohlberg, Carol Gilligan (1993) has questioned its masculine orientation to project autonomy as the ultimate goal against what she finds in women's morality, which is guided by a "web of networks," or interconnectedness with others. Similarly, communities of color have been found to value group membership over inculcating individuality, as with Asian American families. This group orientation has been helpful in promoting academic success through educational practices such as study groups in college. It is possible that this cultural practice is not simply intrinsic to Asian Americans, but also arises from their response to their specific position in race relations, as indicated earlier.

As a response to multiculturalism's systematic critique of Eurocentrism in education, defenders of the latter, such as Lynne Cheney, Allan Bloom, and William Bennett, shift the focus away from Western culture's universality to its superior specificity. From their perspective, admitting to Western culture's particularity does not necessitate abandoning its claims to superiority. Fundamentally, the argument remains the same: Eurocentric culture is superior, universally or specifically. In this reframing, White racial superiority admits that White cultural ways arose from determined conditions, like those of everyone else, but its method of dealing with its environment accomplishes greater advancements. Its focus and cultural premium on liberty, justice, and law and order are indeed accomplishments in their own right, but the historical record has shown its inability to extend these same rights to people of color. They are human rights afforded to Whites, whom the racial contract defines as humans.

From enslavement, to immigrant rights, to full inclusive citizenship in all its forms, it appears that Western entitlements are reserved for Westerners, a right reserved for Whites. In educational terms, cultural enlightenment has become a double-edged sword for students of color as they experience its enforced version through, for example, Indian boarding schools, or it is sometimes withheld from them as in the case of African slaves. To call it assimilation is to underestimate the cultural violence that accompanies it, sometimes literally, such as the struggle to integrate schools in the South, which met stiff resistance from White southerners. From Mississippi to Alabama, the attempt to integrate Blacks in K–12 and university settings during the 1960s was a dangerous process. Whites practiced violence or made threats against the Black students to prevent them from attending these schools. Now a protected right, Black attendance in public schools showcases the importance of education as a site of race struggle.

Language and Culture

One of the central elements of culture is language practice. It is the medium through which a people come to voice in at least a couple ways. Language is the medium through which social groups communicate with one another. This would have been important enough, but language is also the way by which these groups establish meaning, without which they lack cohesion and cultural solidarity. It is not simply what words mean that we stress here, but the entire way that a common language provides a group with its sense of community and establishes a common base of understanding. Moreover, it is a mechanism responsible for their survival as a group, for it provides a worldview that gives rise to a sense of unique selfhood, a sense of order in a complex world, and a sense of belonging and rootedness.

As a symbolic system, language establishes meaning amidst the pressures of everyday life, giving it shape and direction. It would not be difficult to argue that language is the distinguishing feature of humanity, something that separates humans from animals. Taken too far, this distinction may lead to the dehumanization of people born with linguistic challenges, treating them as sub-humans. Or, as has been the case with race, European languages represent the apex of human civilization that the rest of the world tries to equal. These dangers notwithstanding, language is a significant human accomplishment, a thing of beauty.

Language is intimate with racism. Most of the daily, hurtful forms of racism take place on the level of language through epithets, insults, and micro-aggressions, like subtle forms of paternalism. In addition, race relations filter into every aspect of society, including the grammar, meanings, and structure of its dominant language. For example, the title of "American" is saturated with meanings that prevent certain groups from being included in it. Asian Americans are perceived as forever foreign, sometimes regardless of how many generations they may represent. Latino citizenship status is a continuing struggle and the DREAM Act (Development and Relief for the Education of Alien Minors) is only the latest chapter in trying to incorporate Latinos with citizenship rights. Perhaps the most poignant is the case of Native Americans, who have become estranged from their own land. Last, when the "founding fathers" claimed that people were equal under the eyes of the law, it obviously excluded slaves. The definition of "American" also excludes Canadians and Mexicans when that term is used to represent an entire continent that in reality includes non-U.S. nations.

Language is critical to group and individual development, something not lost on colonizers, who sought to impose their language on the colonized. One of these methods is education, which has always been part of the cultural component of colonization (Leonardo & Matias, 2012). From the Philippines to the Falkland Islands, language conversion meant that the natives underwent re-education in the dominant race's language. Often, as in the case of the Filipinos, the earliest teachers were priests, so religion, language, and colonial education were bound up with each other. This process was not seamless and indigenous people often exerted their own (lesser) power over their education, giving rise to hybridized schooling experiences that represent a blend of the colonizer's intent and the ability of the colonized to resist it. In the case of the Philippines, language imposition was the preferred and traditional method, but in other places, a colonial bilingualism, which incorporated indigenous languages but patronized them, was colonialism's *modus operandi*. Currently, administrative colonialism and traditional colonies have been dismantled, but coloniality continues, albeit in new forms. That is, just as the transparency of race power by the name of "White supremacy" has surely faded, Whites' linguistic superiority and race privilege continue.

Today, apart from the most obvious manifestation of the colonial relation with Native Americans, it would seem anachronistic to discuss colonialism as alive and well in the United States. And for the most part, this impression would be accurate. However, other than to the most naïve

Americans, a colonial relation between a dominant White race and subordinate minority races forms the basis for certain educational interactions, such as the derogation of African American language varieties and the language divide for Latinos between their home and school culture. Therefore, a colonial lens is still appropriate as a way to analyze and understand the language policies that affect minority students.

Macedo (2000) has called the English-only movement an expression of colonialism based on its similarity with traditional colonizer–colonized interactions around language where the former imposes its linguistic will upon the latter, often through appeals to objectivity and science. In trend-setting states, like California, where Proposition 227 (1998) all but outlaws bilingual programs in public schools and returns educators to a pre-*Lau* era of incomprehensible education for immigrant students, anti-bilingual sentiments portray Latinos and some Asian students as intransigent with respect to the language of instruction. Proposition 227 includes a waiver, allowing parents of English Language Learners (ELLs) to argue for appropriate language instruction for their children. Be that as it may, when California voters approved Proposition 227, they struck a blow at the legitimacy of learning in languages other than English.

Rather than target educational structures, laws like Proposition 227 project an image that immigrant children are the problem. In other states, like Arizona, where Ethnic Studies programs face their most difficult challenges, and where the nation's immigration policy is closely watched, teachers face social pressures to report suspected undocumented students. In fact, it would not be unreasonable to argue that the United States, unlike its Canadian neighbor to the north, is unlikely to foster bilingualism any time soon without a fundamental shift in language politics. This is paradoxical in light of the predictions of a rapidly changing demographic (Banks, 2004), where it is generally agreed that by the year 2050, in states like California and Texas, Whites will dip below 50 percent and Latinos will become the largest minority group. The 2012 presidential election demonstrated the impact of a growing demographic of Latino voters, for whom immigration policy is an issue of particular concern. Put another way, language policy continues to be a racially charged issue and schools have become one of its battlegrounds.

It is a well-researched phenomenon that immigrant children who speak languages other than English face psycho-social challenges that are subtle but profound. For example, as intermediaries between their mainly English-speaking schools and non-English-dominant households, bilingual students function as young translators between home and school cultures. Probably too immersed in this process to understand completely their experience, which produces levels of anxiety, these students are linguistic border crossers in their daily life. Unlike English-only speakers, bilingual students have to assume roles that are usually reserved for adults. As a result, they are forced to mature rather quickly, causing stress.

To make matters worse, as Chapter 1 suggests, they confront public representations of themselves as somehow resistant to learning English, as if the bilingual agenda is not about learning *two* languages, including English. Again, they are the problem, not the ineffective bilingual programs that could benefit from a dual perspective where second language learning is a burden shared between English-dominant and non-English-dominant students. Children of immigrants and second-generation minority students experience these tensions in their daily lives, in one unreconciled body—too much of color for public schools and in the process of becoming too American (read: becoming culturally White) in their own homes.

The research on bilinguals provides incontrovertible evidence for at least two important facts. One, learning a second language is not compromised by the existence of a first language, as if the brain were a restaurant with limited occupancy. Instead, it is more likely that the brain grows stronger analytically the more languages it assimilates. How many languages and what the tipping point happens to be is outside the scope of this book; whatever the number, two languages do not seem to approach the limit. It is not the case that the first language occupies a limited space with which the second language competes or interferes.

In addition, primary language skills are known to transfer to second-language learning. This phenomenon is plain enough to understand for any high school or college student who learns a foreign language, wherein even a general understanding of the first language's grammar aids in learning the structure of the second language. Or to use a sports analogy, excelling in football, other than as a form of time investment, does not seem to lessen an athlete's chances of developing a good bat swing.

Second, there is much evidence that suggests that bilinguals learn best and advance their academic English, which is differentiated from basic English skills, through strong bilingual programs that both preserve their primary language and disabuse them of the social burden of being the keepers of bilingualism. Regarding the latter, bilingualism becomes a shared agenda with English-only learners and not the burden of ELLs. Seen through the prism of language, culturally relevant education is a school agenda, not the attempt to "fix" immigrant children. It is presented as an opportunity for mutual understanding. If this sketch represents an accurate picture of research on bilingualism, it poses the question as to why more schools do not take up strong versions of bilingual education. This does not minimize the various resources, money or otherwise, that must be organized to create a successful bilingual program. But based on what looks like overwhelming research-based evidence to support bilingualism for ELLs, what guides the English-only movement? Although the English-only movement represents a more extreme, conservative agenda, the United States is unarguably a monolingual nation where English is the unofficial language.

Based on a pair of essays written by Donaldo Macedo (1993) and Diane Ravitch (1993) and collected in the book, *Taking Sides*, on the question of bilingualism and politics, educators are provided with a clue. Whereas former Assistant Secretary of Education Ravitch argued that language education is a matter of instruction and pedagogy, Paulo Freire's former translator Macedo insisted that it is a matter of politics. Based on the evidence that strong bilingual programs are more pedagogically sound than more additive approaches to bilingualism or English-only instruction, Macedo's analysis suggested that political ideology drives the move away from bilingualism.

Undoubtedly, isolating bilingualism frames cultural struggle in a particular direction that centers the experiences of Latino or Asian American students. There is some truth to this, but it is not a zero sum game. Language practices, and therefore language politics, affect all groups. The Ebonics debate that culminated in Oakland, California, public schools during the 1990s is one such case. Its proponents legitimated Ebonics as a language and promoted its use as a bridge to standard English. They made a case for Ebonics as a second language, not unlike Spanish, thus making Oakland schools that boasted high numbers of Ebonics speakers available for Title VII monies and associated bilingual funds.

Though seen by some as stretching the definition of bilingualism, which in its classical conception means languages other than English (to some,

Ebonics equates with Black English), the Ebonics case brings public attention to Black communities' appeal to enter Ebonics into a primarily English–Spanish, secondarily English–Asian languages, domain. Some have argued that Ebonics is not English, but a Niger–Congo dialect (Smith, 1998), based on its grammatical structure; in essence, it is an African language superimposed with English words. The Ebonics debate is driven by several agendas, one of which is to use language as the basis for a culturally relevant education. Although the Oakland experiment ultimately failed, it broadens conceptions of what it means to be bilingual.

The Costs of Culturally Irrelevant Education

A culturally non-relevant education produces several effects, and a lower achievement rate is only one, albeit the most obvious, of them. When students sense that schooling is foreign to their way of understanding, they receive the not so subtle message that their school is not interested in them. They end up feeling like spectators or visitors in a situation that tolerates, but does not welcome, their presence. Thus, they lose interest in school. They learn this message through various mechanisms, not the least of which is the atmosphere that, according to Geneva Gay (2000), does not care for them. As also explained in Chapter 1, they study a curriculum that fails to reflect them. They suffer at least two strikes against them.

In this predicament, students predictably develop either a coping strategy of "playing along" in order to avoid detection or they resist publicly, which puts them at risk of disciplinary measures that are harsher for students of color even when White students behave in a similar manner. Either way, minorities may disengage from school culture because they perceive it as "not for them." The majority of educators would frown upon this result, let alone encourage it. It is not their intention that is in question here, but the practices that are in place culturally to marginalize students of color.

For example, in Angela Valenzuela's (1999) research, an appropriate education for Mexican American students involves attention to their priority for a culturally grounded schooling experience that does not force them to choose between individual success and familial connection. For Valenzuela's participants, *educaçion* is a process that acknowledges family networks and cultivating them, not separating from them. This stands in stark contrast to mainstream, or culturally non-relevant, education that values and promotes autonomy, all the while constructing it as a universal part of human development. Often, this kind of cultural bias goes undetected and becomes an arbitrary standard.

Valenzuela's research (1999) called this pretense of objectivity into question by contextualizing schooling within the cultural lens of Mexican American families. As a result, she unearthed an existing "subtractive education" for many immigrant as well as U.S.-born children, which takes away from, rather than adds, to their self-concept. To make matters worse, researchers have found that the longer Mexican American students stay in U.S. public schools, the worse they perform, the more disconnection from their families they develop, and the lower regard they exhibit toward their own social group, language practices, and culture.

The counterpoint could be that they are assimilating toward mainstream culture so the distance they develop from their ethnic culture is a logical outcome of this process. The problem with that interpretation is that neither they nor Whites believe that Mexicans are becoming White. To illustrate the point, in a 1954 Supreme Court case (Martinez, 1997), Hernandez, a Mexican defendant, argued that his criminal case was unfairly tried because of an all-White jury. The court rejected the appeal based on the fact that Mexicans were considered legally White; therefore he was indeed judged by his White peers. Although this case shows that Mexicans may have been legally White in the past, they are not socially White. They face racial discrimination and cultural backlash as targeted Others, evidenced by anti-immigrant trends in Arizona and other states. They cannot simply blend into Whiteness.

Culturally relevant or responsive education requires that educators care for their minority students. Valenzuela's (1999) version of caring departed from an otherwise general version of it by defining what it means to care, while taking account of students' culture and not regardless of it. This means that caring is not primarily an attitude toward students who remain as ideas, but who are living, feeling beings in the classroom. They are not simply facsimiles of their racial group, despite the fact that they embody its cultural mores and tendencies. It suggests that an effective pedagogy does not regard minority students as either universal human beings outside of culture, or merely particular ones who are mirrors of it. The first perspective forgets their historical nature as specific human beings and the second stereotypes them.

Instead, a proper measure of respect for culture recognizes students' specificity as members of communities with the right to retain their individual uniqueness. It does not deny them membership in a cultural or racial group, but allows the possibility for bi- or multiculturalism— at once a member of a specific ethno-racial community and a general, public life. Geneva Gay (2000) is helpful again when she insists that culturally relevant caring is less a sentiment or feeling and more a social practice. It shows up in educators' behaviors and demeanor toward students of color and their families. When White teachers expect less from minority students because of a lower regard for their capacity to understand, let alone to excel, teachers reinforce their presumed cultural superiority and their students' inferiority. As a result, they do not challenge these students and fulfill the prophecy that leads to their academic mediocrity. When they insist that immigrant children should assimilate the dominant culture, they underestimate the difficulties as well as the benefits of learning to live in two cultures and the unfairness in asking students to abandon one for the other. Whites or Euro-Americans may reason that many of them have lost their native ethnic cultures to adopt American culture and now ask the same of minority students. There are several reasons why comparing White assimilation processes with those for minorities is faulty.

1. It is premised on the assumption that the same outcome awaits Mexicans, Blacks, and Asians who assimilate as it did for White ethnics, like the Irish, Italians, Poles, or Jews. Because the former groups cannot easily blend into White society like the latter, at least phenotypically, membership into the White race does not represent their ultimate destiny. In effect, minorities are asked to relinquish their culture without the trade-off (or up?) that resulted with White ethnic assimilation. That is, White ethnic cultural loss was compensated with membership into the White race. But no such promise is rendered for people of color. It is a loss experienced without a racial trade-up.

2. It does not acknowledge the cultural hazing process that assimilation has become. In other words, the reasoning is that if White ethnics lost their culture in order to assimilate, then minorities should undergo the same process. To the extent that White ethnics have acquiesced to, or were forced to accept, the process of cultural loss, it does not recommend it as a general principle for living in a pluralist society like the United

States. That is, it does not follow that because White ethnics had their culture educated out of them, this was a justified process in the end. If this is accurate, then it is also not acceptable for minorities, and cultural hazing is not a sound process for schools.

3. Most teachers understand the importance of utilizing students' previous knowledge. "Start from where they are" is a hymn teachers often sing. Culturally relevant education affirms this basic value as part of an efficacious pedagogical system. It suggests starting with culture from a position of strength for academic understanding, rather than a deterrent to it. Minority students may experience mobility through assimilation, which has been arguable in the case of Mexican American students, but it is useful to question what kind of "success" educators should promote.

None of this discussion implies that instituting culturally relevant education guarantees student success. There are too many variables that have an impact on education within a racialized system, and this book only takes up six of those. In addition, there are numerous extra-educational issues that schools are either unprepared for or ill-equipped to address, such as chronic family joblessness or poor mental health. These problems may not be appropriate for schools to address. There are many problems that schools did not create and therefore could not solve, such as economic crises or global instability, both of which affect education. Cultural relevance may have to admit to some of its own limitations, which is why culture begins relevant schooling. Race reform in schools does not end there. That said, it is in the schools' power to address those sets of problems they have a large hand in creating, such as an educational process that remains only marginally relevant to students of color. Culturally relevant school reform is then warranted.

Multiculturalism and anti-racist education have gone a long way to address these problems, but there is still much about schooling that passes as "good education" or "universally accepted" ways of conduct even when it is grounded in the particularities of White or Euro-American under-standings. Individualism and the search for absolute truths are often at odds with non-mainstream students' cultural repertoire, whose group or familial affiliations remain strong, or for whom truth is a matter of partial perspec-tives. In more mundane cases, encouraging behaviors such as looking adults in the eye and other leveling of relationships between children and teachers run counter to Native and Asian American culture. The African American narrative style of communication is indirect and filled with details before getting to the point, appearing superfluous to White teachers' sensibilities. In all, educators' failure to admit the cultural basis of educational processes perpetuates racism. Minority students are blamed for being a particular way, which confuses them or they begin to blame themselves for being inadequate.

On the other hand, enacting the power of culturally relevant education for children of color is tantamount to admitting that White children have received a culturally relevant education all these years. It is not an argument that suggests failing White students, but broadening education to become more relevant to minority students' cultural understandings. Experiences in Historically Black Colleges and Universities (HBCUs) have revealed that in places like Howard University, students learn curricula, navigate the school climate, and experience classroom pedagogies that raise their self-esteem and self-efficacy, much like White students in mainly White colleges and universities. Although HBCUs exist within a broader racial market wherein a Howard degree must compete against a Harvard degree, necessitating a more expansive racial analysis about broader structures of race, the point is that culturally relevant education does not sacrifice excellence for ethnic content. Cultural relevance is part of academic relevance.

Study Questions

1. With whose cultural sensibilities does the educational content appear compatible?

2. Which cultural values are constructed as universal human values in the textbooks, classroom materials, or evaluation of students?

3. In cases where human values are named and specified to stem from identifiable racial groups, which ones are valorized, tolerated, or denigrated?

4. Which pedagogical practices in the classroom overlap with which student communities' existing cultural understanding?

5. Which cultural orientations seem to require little to no justification as part of daily classroom interactions, and which ones seem to require justification or are considered disruptive to "normal" school values?

6. Which student groups appear to be disengaged with school material at the level of cultural resonance or relevance?

7. What are the teachers' and administrators' dominant cultural orientations or values at your school?

Selected Readings

Baker, C. & Hornberger, N. (2001). *An introductory reader to the writings of Jim Cummins*. Cleveland, OH: Multilingual Matters Ltd.

Banks, J. (2004). Teaching for social justice, diversity, and citizenship in a global world. *The Educational Forum, 68*, 289–298.

Bloom, B. (1999). The search for methods of instruction. In A. Ornstein & L. Behar (Eds.), *Contemporary issues in curriculum* (pp. 209–226). 2nd Ed. Boston, MA: Allyn and Bacon.

Delpit, L. (1995). *Other people's children*. New York: The New Press.

Fanon, F. (1967). *Black skin white masks*. C. Markmann (Trans.). New York: Grove Press. Originally published in 1952.

Gay, G. (2000). *Culturally responsive teaching: Theory, research, and practice*. New York: Teachers College Press.

Gilligan, C. (1993). *In a different voice: Psychological theory and women's development*. Boston, MA: Harvard University Press.

Howard, T. (2010). *Why race and culture matter in schools*. New York: Teachers College Press.

Kohlberg, L. (1999). The cognitive-developmental approach to moral education. In A. Ornstein & L. Behar (Eds.), *Contemporary issues in curriculum* (pp. 163–175). 2nd Ed. Boston, MA: Allyn and Bacon.

Ladson-Billings, G. (1995). Toward a theory of culturally relevant pedagogy. *American Educational Research Journal, 32*(3), 465–491.

Leonardo, Z. & Matias, C. (2012). Betwixt and between colonial and postcolonial mentality: The critical education of Filipino Americans. In D. Maramba & R. Bonus (Eds.), *The "other students": Filipino Americans, education, and power* (pp. 3–18). Charlotte, NC: Information Age Publishing.

Macedo, D. (1993). English only: The tongue-tying of America. In J. Noll (Ed.), *Taking sides* (pp. 263–272). 7th Ed. Guilford, CT: The Dushkin Publishing Group.

Macedo, D. (2000). The colonialism of the English-only movement. *Educational Researcher, 29*(3), 15–24.

Martinez, G. (1997). Mexican-Americans and whiteness. In R. Delgado & J. Stefancic (Eds.), *Critical white studies* (pp. 210–213). Philadelphia, PA: Temple University Press.

Portes, A. & Rumbaut, R. (2001). *Legacies.* Berkeley: University of California Press.

Ravitch, D. (1993). Politicization and the schools: The case of bilingual education. In J. Noll (Ed.), *Taking sides* (pp. 254–262). 7th Ed. Guilford, CT: The Dushkin Publishing Group.

Smith, E. (1998). What is Black English? What is Ebonics? In T. Perry & L. Delpit (Eds.), *The real Ebonics debate: Power, language, and the education of African-American children* (pp. 49–58). Boston, MA: Beacon Press.

Sue, S. & Okazaki, S. (1995). Asian American educational achievements: A phenomenon in search of an explanation. In D. Nakanishi & T. Nishida (Eds.), *The Asian American educational experience* (pp. 133–145). New York: Routledge.

Valdes, G. (2001). *Learning and not learning English.* New York: Teachers College Press.

Valenzuela, A. (1999). *Subtractive schooling: US-Mexican youth and the politics of caring.* Albany, NY: State University of New York Press.

School–Community Relations and Racism

The School–Community Nexus

As the previous chapter's beginning story makes clear, schools both serve and are part of communities. They are nested in complex relations with students, their families, and a network of people represented in the surrounding area in the form of businesses, neighborhood organizations, and the division of labor. Most schools rely on good relations with their constituencies, something most schools seek, and some brag about, as early as orientation nights for prospective parents and students. They depend on parents' willingness to reinforce school values in the home, provide volunteer work in the classroom, or attend school events, such as Open House or fundraising opportunities, like the popular auction nights held at many public schools. However, because race and culture represent difficulties, sometimes clashes, between schools and communities, educators struggle with incorporating people of color into the educational process as full partners and participants. A racial gap between schools and the minority communities they serve inevitably opens up. The racial divide between schools and their community is the concern of this chapter.

If we take a serious look at the concept of community, it takes on a fuller meaning. Through ethnographies of schools, or in-depth studies of their culture, readers learn that a community's relationship with schools is arguably forged for decades, setting in motion decisions that make its current institutional form seem natural. Because a school's existence is located in a web of other institutional forms, such as job industries and workplaces, it is intimate with the local context in a way that initially escapes educators' understanding. In other words, schools are located in the political economy of cities. A school is entangled with the city's economic development as well as the political apparatus, including school boards, which are responsible for policies that have an impact on a school's, sometimes an entire district's, limits for possible action and self-determination. Of course, these social conditions change over the decades and change a school's course or direction. In dire situations, such as the schools in Newark, New Jersey or East St. Louis, Illinois, turning around struggling school districts becomes a Herculean, though not impossible, task. Like the decades of disinvestment that some schools have suffered, it would take a similar, long-term investment to lift failing schools out of their moribund status.

With respect to race, demographics alone speak to the basic struggle between schools and communities. With the challenge of integration, schools are called on to respect the multiple forms of ethnic and racial diversities that walk into the classroom. But in the largest states, like California, New York, and Texas, a constant stream of initiatives and propositions testify to the tension-filled relationship between schools and communities. In every decade since the 1980s, California has attempted to deal with its population of color, often targeting Latinos, through constrictions such as Proposition 187 (1994), which limited undocumented citizens' access to social services, like prenatal care and education; Proposition 227 (1998), which struck a blow to the legitimacy of bilingual education; and Proposition 209 (1996), which outlawed affirmative action. While Latinos are welcomed for their ability to provide basic labor in the service economy, their integration is simultaneously curtailed by xenophobic attitudes that perceive them as difficult to assimilate into American culture.

Among the acknowledged racial groups, Latinos register the lowest high school graduation rate (Solorzano & Yosso, 2000). Out of 100 Latino students entering the educational pipeline at elementary level, only one eventually enters a doctoral program. This rate may be broken up to account for ethnic differences among Latinos, such as the low attrition rate for Cubans compared to their Mexican counterparts. One confounding factor in this comparison is that Cubans enter the United States with a higher class status, particularly the wave following the fall in 1959 of Cuba's leader, Batista, when compared with Mexicans, a large portion of whom are incorporated into the service or working-class economy. That said, as a racial group, Latinos continue to struggle with a U.S. education system that has yet to take advantage of their communities' offerings. Moreover, the longer Latino youth enroll in U.S. schools, the more their educational attainment drops, suggesting that the more they are "assimilated," the more they experience "subtractive education," as pointed out in Chapter 2.

Subtractive education describes the process that Mexican American students experience when their cultural mores are not central to or respected in their education. In effect, schools force fit them into an existing school culture that goes against their own cultural understanding. Whereas schools should arguably take advantage of the cultural resources present in these students' communities, schools perceive their culture through the lens of a "deficit." Cultural orientations of Latinos, such as group advancement, prioritization of family, and a collaborative rather than competitive spirit do not mesh well with public education's focus on autonomy and instrumentalism. As a result, Mexican American students experience distance, if not a contradiction, between their schooling and community life. Or worse, they are perceived as resistant to assimilation or as contradictory to American culture.

Being a "Problem" and the Culture of Poverty

At the beginning of the 20th century, W. E. B. Du Bois wrote treatises on African American life, arguably captured best by his classic text, *The Souls of Black Folk* (1989/1904). Particularly in Chapter 2 on "spiritual strivings," Du Bois asked a question that has since haunted the educational scene. To Blacks, he asked, "How does it feel to be a problem?" Meant partly as an ironic statement about Black marginalization under the thumb of White power, which was the real problem, Du Bois accurately apprehended what life is like when one is *perceived* by the dominant race as a problem.

Offering poignant and lyrical prose about the twoness of Black existence, whereby Blacks live through their own values but function under the imposition of White values, Du Bois coined the phrase "double consciousness" to describe the gift as well as the burden of being Black in the United States. As testament, Du Bois offered his own educational journey from grade school to graduate school at Harvard as the first Black person eventually to earn a doctoral degree from the nation's top university, where he sensed his peculiar place as an interloper despite his intellectual talents, achievements, and resolve. As part of a perceived "problem," Du Bois becomes a symbol for a larger phenomenon when entire racialized communities, like Blacks in this instance, become a problem to be fixed. Education has always functioned in this double-edged way for minorities. Eager to prove their mettle, people of color also experience racial discrimination in the nation's institutions like schools.

In schools, communities of color become a problem for an educational system that vacillates between assimilating them into Eurocentrism and forsaking them as drains on the system. These are natural responses if educators premise schooling on a sink or swim mentality, otherwise known as the bootstrap philosophy. But educators are more likely to be people who struggle to bridge the cultural gap between what they know or have been trained under, and having the knowledge base to deal effectively with a population different from their own. This dilemma precipitated the need for multiculturalism, a perspective that aims to integrate minority histories and concerns into the official curriculum. For mainstream educators, it represents an attempt to broaden their understanding of non-White groups and gain valuable information, if not insight, about them. Without this knowledge base, teachers fall back on what they know, which, based on the fact that most teachers are White women, means that what Joe Feagin (2009) has called a "White racial frame" becomes teachers' default orientation for understanding. As part of their racial conditioning, White teachers reduce life chances to individual worth and effort. Underachievement is explained as a person or group's shortcoming; they lack something. They underestimate the role of Whites' racial interests to maintain social institutions the way they are, which benefits Whites as a racial group.

Unfortunately, regarding students of color through a deficit lens still persists. This means that despite the best of intentions, teachers may still perceive students of color as lacking certain cultural competencies by virtue of being different or non-mainstream. Its extreme form is summed up with the label of "uneducable," or when students of color are deemed near impossible to educate. This is not only about an individual student's perceived failures, but a way of constructing the racial community in which he or she belongs through an impoverished lens. The student becomes the target of competencies to which he or she must be provided access, such as valuing education, de-emphasizing immediate gratification, and respecting authority, making the situation ripe with paternalism. It is the students who must change, not the schools.

Students of color are infused with cultural practices that will, it is hoped, position them for success in education and beyond. This comes with good sense as schools should prepare the most disadvantaged students for possibilities of success. Its limitation arrives when we consider education's civilizing mission, of changing "them" to become more like "us." An alternative education is one that fundamentally changes both Whites and minorities when their worldviews mutually influence one another, making for a bi-directional, bicultural process. This is success that incorporates the minority students' previous knowledge and pre-existing comprehension of the world.

This process of socialization is not without good intentions, as various programs, such as the Knowledge Is Power Program (KIPP), work with working-class students of color to assimilate middle-class practices, such as building study habits, professionalism, and comportment. Programs like KIPP are often found in urban cities teeming with people of color, many of whom have a bleak educational future. Indeed, working-class culture has its own limitations, which are part of the class existence in which the culture is embedded, such as a limited vocabulary when compared to the middle class and low participation in political processes like voting. Exposing working-class children to habits that put them in a better position for school success seems a logical step. Some of these students struggle with limited prospects for the future, some are headed for the school-to-prison pipeline. In either scenario, they become a dilemma to be solved, a mindset that is difficult to break once it is established.

At the same time that Du Bois was writing about African American experience within the color line, White social scientists began a long tradition of scholarship with respect to Black culture. Although Du Bois was arguably interpreting the color line itself as the *real source of the problem*, social scientists since Du Bois have shifted the problem to be something internal to Black culture. Rather than locate the culprit in structural racism, depictions of Black culture became understood through the lens of pathology, such that it comprised a set of cultural strategies marked by criminality, irresponsibility, and hypersexuality. With this idea having staying power through the phrase "culture of poverty," Blacks are ossified in the educational imagination as lacking virtues that would otherwise assist in their school success.

Originally conceived as responses to economic marginalization, the culture of poverty is naturalized as Black culture. It is not an effect of a larger problem, but the cause of it. Whereas participating in illicit economies, like the drug industry, or taking short cuts rather than investing in schooling were once conceived as coping strategies, they have since been understood (Glazer & Moynihan, 1970) as having their own autonomy from economic poverty and instead represent Black culture itself. Rather than stemming from poverty, Black culture is instead impoverished. The effect has become the cause. Because poverty and the accompanying racial ghettoization of Blacks are pervasive, this image ultimately covers the majority of Black communities and implicates all Black people on one level or another. The culture of poverty effectively becomes something about them and not about the racialized economy that gives rise to their cultural practices.

Schools are not immune from this mindset. The culture of poverty argument is prevalent in education as one of the favored explanations for students of color who fail to achieve. As the phrase suggests, communities mired in poverty possess a culture. Its profile includes low priority placed on schooling, informed by a low value placed on delayed gratification, or sacrificing present desires for future returns. Because of the inability to invest in future prospects that lead to more productive or secure lives, this kind of deficiency sets in motion a life of struggle. There is some reality to this claim, which should not be minimized. The condition of poverty creates a culture designed to deal with its limitations. The debate is not whether or not a culture of poverty exists; it does. The analysis hinges on this culture's relationship with perpetuating the condition of poverty that produces it.

Urban ethnographies have confirmed cultural practices of the Black poor, replete with informal economies, higher rates of crime, and a life of survival guided by brutal necessities. Other research has found that a certain oppositional culture pervades Black students who consider doing well in school as "acting White" and therefore to be avoided. These patterns are real, but how educators might explain them is not a straightforward issue. The "culture of poverty" line of thought affects schools' relationships with minority communities because it drives educators' understanding of them, thereby defining the nature of the problem and possible solutions to it. In short, if the problem is the communities' culture, then it stands to reason that it must be changed. However, culture is arguably an outcome of the structural condition of race and the poverty to which it gives rise. It is a combination of limitations that are reproduced at the level of culture as well as coping mechanisms created to survive them. The culture of poverty may be real and helps reproduce the cycle of being poor, but it does not explain the structure of racism that places limits on people of color's choices for mobility.

In the 1970s, there was an attempt by social scientists to recast these strategies as people's creative ways to adapt to their limitations, putting a more productive spin on them. For example, in the case of Black boys and men, a particular style of street savvy portrays them in a more positive light as adaptive and having social imagination. These efforts notwithstanding, it appears that the culture of poverty argument remains strong decades later. In the case of communities of color, who disproportionately make up poor neighborhoods, a cultural deficit model portrays them as lacking in certain competencies or virtues. Countering this tendency requires that educators deliberately shift their orientation toward communities of color. This includes reconsidering their culture as a source of knowledge, strength, and having something to offer schools.

Cultural Capital Arguments

Another species of arguments explaining the relationship between schools and communities of color comes from Pierre Bourdieu's sociological concept of "cultural capital" (Bourdieu, 1977; Bourdieu & Passeron, 1990/1977). Originally embedded in the context of French aristocracy and the high status afforded to their culture, Bourdieu's study explained the public "distinction" accompanying French aristocratic culture in public life. From refined social taste, to abstract language practice, and attachment to classical forms of education, high culture is given prestige and status when compared to the common culture. Having control of material wealth, French aristocrats also possess the favored culture, which they transmit to their children, whose social position is secured and reproduced in the process. By tracing the conversion of economic resources to cultural power, Bourdieu made it possible to talk about the transmission of skills, habits, and dispositions already central to the schooling process. For certain populations, the match between home and school culture appears almost seamless.

In U.S. public education, cultural reproduction happens when school rituals cater to middle-class sensibilities, such as preferring language practices characterized by "expanded codes" over those with "limited codes"

(Bernstein, 1977). For instance, middle-class language use between adults and children is characterized by adult explanations and encouraging children to inquire into their meanings, rather than the unspoken shared assumptions between adults and children common in working-class homes. In short, middle-class children are encouraged to ask for information, whereas working-class kids function in a linguistic environment where adults assume shared meanings with them, needing little extrapolation. The middle class expands children's linguistic repertoire and the working class tends to limit it. From the sheer number of words learned in early childhood during routine interactions in everyday life, compared to working-class kids, middle-class children live in an academically enriched environment that closely resembles school culture, preparing them even before they enter the school. By the age of five, middle- class kids know several thousand more words than their working-class counterparts. Because we also know that the working class is comprised disproportionately of racial minorities, race analysis helps paint a clearer picture of the disparity.

These cultural codes create different social environments where middle-class kids' interactions are filled with literacy events in the home. These practices, such as turning even mundane experiences like reading food labels into educational ones, correcting children's grammar and diction to enforce standard English, and quizzing them with mathematics factoids around the dinner table, mirror activities in the school system and contribute to school preparedness. These daily, cultural habits advance middle-class children's literacy and mathematics skills as much as the more acknowledged importance of bedtime reading routines. Children are encouraged to reflect on or confront their feelings and explain them by writing in their journals; middle-class parents are known to seek out toys that have educational value; and kids are taught negotiation skills both with other children and adults. In all these facets, middle-class kids enter kindergarten well ahead of their working-class counterparts. For many of the latter, catching up never happens and the gap is even wider by high school.

There are at least two reasons for these cultural patterns. First, because working-class communities are limited in terms of neighborhoods, they traverse a much more limited geography, usually bordered by their local area or parents' workplace. Their sense of space is enclosed. Within this space, working-class children establish complex associations within an extended kinship system, but their social life's spatial boundary is more defined than that of middle-class children who experience a broader set of relations because of their parents' economic and social options. Racially speaking, these developments are direct results of the social isolation resulting from ghettoization and housing segregation. Because schooling is by and large tied to neighborhoods, housing segregation produces school segregation. Although integrated schools exist, because of segregation, most Black children attend schools populated with other Black children.

Second, working-class adults function within a work life guided by a hierarchical structure, and their livelihood is defined by their ability to follow instructions doled out by authority figures. Often, they exercise little control over their job, both in terms of its execution and creative dimensions. They are often deskilled so as to minimize their decision-making power as well as potential mistakes in the labor production process. These work habits translate into cultural dispositions that are then passed on to children whom working-class parents have good reason to think will pursue working-class jobs in the future. As a result, they do their own part in completing the circle of cultural reproduction.

Because public schools favor middle-class values and teachers both embody and inculcate them as middle-class workers, the mechanism for reproducing middle-class culture in schools becomes naturalized, conceived as universally good habits rather than what Bourdieu called the "cultural arbitrary" (Bourdieu & Passeron, 1990/1977) that schools have chosen and promote. To the casual observer, middle-class ways become common sense culture. Deviating from them is to be out of sync with a school's "official culture." While there is much about middle-class culture that recommends itself, such as bedtime reading or encouraging educative mundane interactions, Bourdieu's point was that the class basis for these activities passes unremarkably or unmarked as results of a larger class-based social system defined by an unequal relation of power. Appropriated for a racial analysis, promoting the dominant group's cultural ways to which students of color must adapt has been challenged in the era of multiculturalism.

Although Bourdieu's original intent was to unveil the class dimensions of cultural reproduction, educational scholars have found it to be a powerful explanation for racial minorities' school experiences and have appropriated the framework to explain the process of racial reproduction. Because class issues are implicated in race relations, not the least of which is the disproportionate number of people of color living in poverty, it is a natural, conceptual fit. Although class explanations do not map completely onto race relations, Bourdieu's reproduction theory has proven to be a useful explanation for the maintenance of racism. For instance, many studies that focus on class culture also implicate race. In the United States, there is no neat way to separate class from race relations because they presuppose each other. Although race stratification is commonly understood as a hierarchy along the color line, such that the darker an imagined group, the lower its chances for school success, racism is also the process of subverting a social group's way of life and the imposition of another way of living, feeling, and thinking.

Translating Bourdieu's concept of cultural capital for a racial predicament is the attempt to explain the lower status of communities of color in the schooling process. In short, minority culture does not translate into a form of capital or power within public schools. In the realm of class, working-class parents usually exhibit lower rates of in-school involvement for various reasons, including a) putting their faith in teachers as professionals; b) showing deference to teachers; and c) feeling intimidated by the teachers' use of language and show of knowledge. During parent–teacher conferences, Open House, and public school meetings, such as fundraisers, working-class parents display a consistent pattern of being disenfranchised, even disempowered. Unlike their middle-class counterparts, who exert a tremendous influence on teachers by holding them accountable to their expectations regarding their children's education, parents from modest class backgrounds are comparatively less demanding of teachers and less forthcoming about their expectations. The latter's cultural dispositions, values, and ways of interacting with school authorities do not translate into forms of capital in the institutional setting which they could leverage with their children's teachers.

Often, uneducated, working-class parents lack the bureaucratic knowledge, intellectual background, and institutional navigation skills that influence the direction of public schools, particularly when advocating for their children. As a result, they become marginalized in the processes that determine their children's school life, and therefore life chances. In contrast, middle-class communities are known for advocating on behalf of their children, sometimes even intimidating educators by their professional status, such as parents who are doctors, lawyers, or businesspeople. They possess public assertiveness that schools respect, command with words that persuade authorities, and have impressive social networks that buoy them if they should need assistance. In this case, their culture converts into capital that they "cash in."

In terms of race, parents of color face disparities in status, particularly when we consider the fact that American teachers are overwhelmingly White. Parents of color of any economic class are compromised because of their lower racial standing in society, which negatively affects their ability to influence schools. Already exacerbated by class differences, race disparity becomes a formidable challenge for communities of color. Functioning in a society that conceives of them as a problem, communities of color have uneasy relations with public schools. Here are a few of the symptoms of this relationship.

1. There are significant cultural differences between Whites and families of color. Without providing an exhaustive list, White families typically favor independence, whereas non-Whites value familial ties; the former promote fewer distinctions between children and adults, whereas the latter value clearer separation between the two; and Whites, particularly from the middle class, are known to favor indirect language practices over directives. For instance, in dealings with children, White adults use requests or inquiries to compel students to do their work or stay on task ("Perhaps we could begin our work now?"), whereas adults of color are inclined to use directives with children to accomplish the same ("Let's do our work now.").

2. A common way to marginalize communities of color, which is sometimes more difficult to detect but may be just as damaging, is to regard their worldview or orientation through a deficit perspective. This is a more subtle way to send the message that these families are not valued in school, at least not on an equal footing with White families. It is an updated version of being perceived as a problem when minority participation is not cultivated by schools, let alone invited.

It is possible that, especially considering Bourdieu's explanation above, parents of color neither look forward nor show up to Open House and parent–teacher conferences because they lack the confidence, find these events unwelcoming, or feel intimidated by White teachers. This being plausible if not likely, schools could consider altering the way they conduct these activities, such as offering language translators on site.

It is tempting to eliminate these distinctions and favor a color-blind perspective. Putting aside cultural differences in favor of deracialized or universal human values runs into several difficulties, however, including the insistence that families of color adopt the official culture of the school without making accommodations for them. Or to use Bourdieu's language, White middle-class values become the "cultural arbitrary" that goes undetected as such. Fortunately, most schools, following the lead of multiculturalism, recognize the value of integration whereby diversity has become a valued good.

This transformation does not require White teachers to adopt cultures of color, which is a strategy mired with difficulties, including paternalism. It requires an openness to non-White ways as legitimate even if they may seem strangely different. As is more common, schools expect parents who speak languages other than English, for example, to adopt English as a prerequisite to participating in school processes. When it proves difficult to enact, sometimes parents proficient in a language other than English are blamed as resistant or difficult. This does not suggest that schools show no cultural interest whatsoever; or they may not possess the necessary resources to provide these additional services. On the contrary, these are difficult matters to resolve and funding would go a long way to address them, something that is necessary but not sufficient, as we discuss in Chapter 5. However, without deliberate efforts to ameliorate these conditions because the differences are perceived to be unbridgeable and overwhelming, teachers default to the culture they know best and with which they feel comfortable. This may seem natural, but it will have the tendency to reinforce existing race relations.

Participation in school is one way that educators gauge parental involvement. It is visible, activities are relatively well-defined, and educators exercise control over how it transpires. However, there are forms of parental involvement that are invisible or harder to account for, such as practices in the home. So whereas research on in-school involvement confirms the lower rates of participation by minority families for a range of reasons, their out-of-school practices are harder to observe and become a challenge for researchers and practitioners. For instance, it is indisputable that families of color, whether poor or middle class, are part of social networks. Compared with the White middle class, working-class families of color are not part of formal networks gained through standard work relations. They are more loose and informal, and bartering or trading one service for another is common, such as providing auto care for someone whose car needs fixing in exchange for house repair or an appliance. These relations are indicative of a "funds of knowledge" approach, which we explicate in the next section. Some of these transactions lead to resources that contribute to students' well-being and stability, which are vital to schooling. Moreover, children learn something educative about the importance of managing relations and using resources at their disposal toward productive ends.

Alternative work in education reframes cultural capital arguments that treat minority culture as deficient by emphasizing the "cultural wealth" that communities of color possess. That is, within their own context, minority culture represents a form of resource, where their language is the preferred mode of communication and their mindset the one that carries status. It is a culture with a lower status only when perceived from the outside, such as through mainstream White standards. Instead, viewed from within, minority cultures represent a tradition of strength rather than weakness. In these cultures, teachers find a wealth of resources that are valued by communities of color, but remain largely unrecognized by schools. Even worse, educators perceive them as problematic, leading to opinions that are turned into policies around minority students' uneducability, their communities' apparent lack of priority for education, and parents' lack of involvement in schools.

By shifting their lens, educators discover minority communities' ability to maintain educational aspirations in the face of institutional processes that consistently chip away at them. They persevere despite the daily discouragements. Other resources teachers may expect to find here include minority history, which is communal and vibrant; their language, which retains its vitality; and their families, which are full of tradition and competencies. By broadening arguments about cultural capital to include these forms of cultural wealth, educators may be able to appreciate value in these settings and counter the prevailing deficit orientation regarding racial minorities in schools.

Culture, Power, and a Funds of Knowledge Approach

Understanding the culture of power requires at least two steps. First, teachers must help students of color to demystify the culture of power by knowing how it works. The culture of power is a way of conducting schools in a way that favors Whites as the dominant racial group, but makes the process and outcomes appear natural. It includes promoting certain behaviors and ways of interacting with others. According to Lisa Delpit (1995, p. 24), this cultural power may be characterized in the following ways:

1. Issues of power are enacted in classrooms.

2. There are codes or rules for participating in power.

3. The rules of the culture of power are a reflection of the rules of the culture of those who have power.

4. If you are not already a participant in the culture of power, being told explicitly the rules of that culture makes acquiring power easier.

5. Those with power are frequently least aware of—or least willing to acknowledge—its existence. Those with less power are often most aware of its existence.

Demystifying cultural power may be a way to counteract it, but is also a way to wield power to accomplish other productive ends. In other words, knowing how cultural power works in schools is arguably a way for students to be comfortable when confronted with it, rather than being debilitated or disarmed by it. Such simple practices—like a firm handshake or exuding confidence; or coping with situations like dealing with authority, or asserting oneself in public; or developing political skills—begin to serve previously marginalized students rather than further harming them.

Second, regarding cultural power as a tool that students can use rather than one that disempowers them provides educators with a way of teaching students about relations of power and how to have a healthier relationship with authority in general, whether in the form of school tradition, like the official curriculum, or institutional leaders, like teachers and administrators. Because most people in leadership positions, from principals to work supervisors, are likely to be White, children of color learn to become comfortable in their presence, knowledgeable about their cultural practices, and at ease in dealing with them. If these authorities remain mysterious to students of color, they will probably resist them, some forms of which may further marginalize them. Instead, by knowing how the culture of power works, they learn how to negotiate it rather than being under its sway. The culture of power may then be appropriated and in some cases redirected toward alternative ends. This perspective neither romanticizes nor fears cultural power, but provides a realistic understanding of it.

All of this suggests that communities possess funds of knowledge that serve their needs, gleaned from the human resources and cultural understanding present in them. Unlike Bourdieu's sociology-inspired concept of cultural capital, the concept of funds of knowledge comes from anthropological studies of households as a way of understanding the cultural transactions that transpire in them and the role households play in a larger field of cultural exchange in communities. Rather than explaining social stratification more common to cultural capital arguments, the funds of knowledge approach affirms processes that lead to reciprocity and mutual benefit among its participants. A funds of knowledge approach to minority communities opposes the deficit orientation by considering the worth of people according to their own standards regarding what knowledge is of most worth and value, and not from an external lens that disparages them.

By opening up to other ways of viewing people of color's priorities, like the ultimate goal of education as tied to community relations rather than individual advancement, human connection as valuing relationships over autonomy, and the social functions of knowledge over its mastery, educators begin to appreciate culture from multiple perspectives. In essence, this has been the argument and position of multiculturalism, which is to procure an educational experience that combines different vantage points. But we recognize that cultures exist in context, sometimes even in tension, with other cultures, so understanding them on their own terms becomes challenging. A funds of knowledge approach represents one perspective for accomplishing this task.

A funds of knowledge approach, even at the level of terminology, provides a contrast for the culture of poverty orientation so popular in education. Rather than start from the premise of impoverishment, it begins by affirming the wealth of knowledge that a culture possesses. We note that this approach may already be in place for White communities who are regarded with honor and respect in public schools. Their knowledge is already regarded as a fund rather than a deficit. The funds of knowledge concept is the attempt to broaden this sentiment to include otherwise marginalized students. It matches good intentions with good practice by honoring minorities and pedagogically welcoming their perspectives into the classroom.

Most ideas on sound pedagogy already acknowledge this general strategy—of beginning where students are—but when it comes to cultural competence, good intentions have not always translated into good practice. Black, Latino, Asian American, and Native American knowledge systems have made their way into the official curriculum, but multicultural and anti-racist pedagogy has not been without challenge. This difficulty makes realistic sense because crafting an abstract curriculum that values diversity is one thing, and confronting real students of color in the classroom is another. The first is difficult enough, but the second is comprised of human interaction, involves human volition, and takes a certain political commitment to pull off.

Although using a similar family of metaphors, funds of knowledge should not be confused with the much criticized "banking education" that Paulo Freire first diagnosed. In the latter, racial inequality is exacerbated when students are treated as depositories of knowledge stored until testing, which is ubiquitous for all students in public education in the era of standardization. We will have more to say about this topic in Chapter 6. Here, we note that in most cases, schools with predominantly working-class students of color have fared worse than their White middle-class counterparts on standardized tests. At testing time, the knowledge that was "deposited" into students' minds is "withdrawn," to be traded in for a rating to assess a school's Adequate Yearly Progress (AYP) under the No Child Left Behind Act. Although advancements in the scores are made, the same population is likely still to be left behind as the year 2014 passes, or 12 years from NCLB's authorization, which is the target date for reaching academic proficiency across the nation. In general, educators are not confident that NCLB has approached the goal of ending the achievement gap.

In contrast to "banking education," the funds of knowledge approach is guided by a principle that regards all students as capable learners within a context where knowledge is negotiated rather than transmitted. In this perspective, knowledge is not a "thing" to be passed on, but part of a relationship forged within a community of practice between adults and young people. In other words, knowledge is forged in a relationship and produced in a condition wherein all participants are assumed to be contributors; it is not a possession that resides in the students' heads. If knowledge is traded at all in this approach, it is exchanged for services that lead to the subsistence and survival of a community.

An education guided by funds of knowledge recognizes that students' school life is inherently bound up with their home and community life. As a basis for classroom pedagogy, cultural understandings that originate from households are tapped for their creative and generative functions. For example, because many minority homes are modest and scarcity arguably defines everyday life, students learn to barter early on. They build social networks that serve this need, requiring their persistence to accomplish certain ends. Educators who understand this condition comprehend the full measure of importance given to context, of how Black students, for example, appear circuitous in their narratives when perceived from a White standard of brevity or "getting to the point." As scholars who focus on African American language varieties have pointed out, there is a tendency for Black students to favor a narrative style of talking that winds through streets of descriptions and avenues of details. To a mainstream sensibility, the destination is what counts most. A culturally sensitive approach goes a long way to complicate this preference.

The school–community relationship is a key node in understanding racism in education as well as ways to counteract it. Challenged by a deficit model that regards students of color as problems to be fixed, U.S. schools vacillate between romanticizing and pathologizing them. Concerning the first, students of color are not appreciated for their cultural specificity. Schools deculturalize and strip them of cultural content. Regarding the second, students of color and their families become burdens on the system, making disregarding them that much easier. As this book suggests, educators can do better. On the one hand, understanding cultural power enables them to shine a light on existing practices and how they contribute to marginalization. On the other hand, extending respect to people of color by including their cultures, languages, and values in schooling, especially when they comprise the majority student body in certain contexts, goes a long way in bridging the home–school divide that most educators work so hard to accomplish.

Study Questions

1. What are considered forms of cultural capital in your classroom or those you have observed?

2. Identify the cultural practices, such as language use, that students display for expressing themselves in your classroom?

3. What does it mean to be "educated," according to the students and families you serve? What is your own personal understanding of being "educated"?

4. In what ways is the culture of students of color regarded through a deficit framework in your school?

5. How do you plan to become acquainted with your students' households and what will you do to prepare yourself for this process?

6. What are your preconceptions about your students' homes and what do you expect to learn from them?

7. How do you plan to integrate your school community's funds of knowledge into your pedagogy?

Selected Readings

Bernstein, B. (1977). Social class, language and socialization. In J. Karabel & A. H. Halsey (Eds.), *Power and ideology in education* (pp. 473–486). Oxford, UK: Oxford University Press.

Bourdieu, P. (1977). Cultural reproduction and social reproduction. In J. Karabel & A. H. Halsey (Eds.), *Power and ideology in education* (pp. 487–511). Oxford, UK: Oxford University Press.

Bourdieu, P. & Passeron, J. (1990). *Reproduction in education, society, and culture.* Thousand Oaks, CA: SAGE. First published in 1977.

Delpit, L. (1995). *Other people's children.* New York: The New Press.

Du Bois, W. E. B. (1989). *The souls of black folk.* New York: Penguin Books. First published in 1904.

Feagin, J. (2009). *The White racial frame.* New York: Routledge.

Fordham, S. & Ogbu, J. (1986). Black students' school success: Coping with the "burden of 'acting White'." *Urban Review, 18*(3), 176–206.

Heath, S. B. (1983). *Ways with words.* Cambridge, UK: Cambridge University Press.

Lareau, A. (2003). *Unequal childhoods*. Berkeley, CA: University of California Press.

Lewis, O. (1968). The culture of poverty. In D. P. Moynihan (Ed.), *On understanding poverty: Perspectives from the social sciences* (pp. 187–220). New York: Basic Books.

Moll, L. & Gonzalez, N. (2004). Engaging life: A funds-of-knowledge approach to multicultural education. In J. Banks & C. Banks (Eds.), *Handbook of research on multicultural education* (pp. 699–715). 2nd Ed. San Francisco, CA: Jossey-Bass.

Moll, L. & Greenberg, J. (1990). Creating zones of possibilities: Combining social contexts for instruction. In L. Moll (Ed.), *Vygotsky and education* (pp. 319–348). Cambridge, UK: Cambridge University Press.

Solorzano, D. & Yosso, T. (2000). Toward a critical race theory of Chicana and Chicano education. In C. Tejeda, C. Martinez, & Z. Leonardo (Eds.), *Charting new terrains of Chicana(o)/Latina(o) education* (pp. 35–65). Cresskill, NJ: Hampton Press.[0]

Yosso, T. (2006). *Critical race counterstories along the Chicana/Chicano educational pipeline*. New York: Routledge.

Tracking, Segregation, and Racism

Tracking and segregation are among the most contentious issues in American education. Both separate students into groups, and then direct these groups to different educational opportunities or pathways— some clearly superior to others. Both have long histories, and both have generated enormous conflicts, among researchers, parents, teachers, administrators, and policy makers. Tracking and segregation are widespread and both reduce the options for some groups of students—particularly for African American, Latino, and other racial minority students—at the same time that they may benefit other students. But the extent and mechanisms of tracking and segregation are empirical issues, and we have to know what we are looking for before we can understand them.

This chapter reviews many types of tracking and segregation, and clarifies that these practices are much more widespread than many people think. The practices include within-school tracking, which is the usual conception; among-school tracking; tracking in postsecondary as well as elementary and secondary education; and tracking due to residential segregation. There are positive as well as negative pathways, and—despite the common view that all tracking undermines equity and opportunities for racial minorities—there are some conditions under which different pathways can enhance equity. So we have to understand precisely what tracking does before we can take positions for and against it.

The writing about tracking, some of which is cited under "Selected Readings," does not often incorporate material on racial desegregation and segregation. The term "segregation" almost always reflects racial and ethnic segregation, while tracking encompasses many more meanings. But the two operate in quite similar fashions; indeed, tracking has been called "second generation segregation," and it has sometimes been used as a substitute for older patterns of racial segregation. Therefore this chapter includes a section on racial segregation to show how similar it is to the mechanisms of tracking.

Tracking in K–12 Education

Tracking takes several different forms in K–12 schooling. It is worth explaining each one because the causes—and therefore the remedies—are quite different.

Within-school Tracking

Perhaps the most common form of tracking, and the pattern which critics like Jeannie Oakes find most objectionable, is within-school tracking. This refers to the practice of dividing students in the same grade into groups and then assigning them to different classrooms and teachers.

In middle schools and sometimes in elementary schools, tracking is usually based on "ability," or prior performance, including test scores and teacher recommendations. As we will see, tracking decisions are based on objective as well as subjective reasoning—test scores on the one hand, teachers' racialized perceptions of students on the other. In the past, the most common form of tracking in high schools has been based on presumed occupations, where college-bound students in the academic or "honors" track are separated from those in a "general" track of watered-down academic offerings, or from other students allocated to vocational tracks of some sort. These include retail and wholesale trade, agriculture, home economics for girls, industrial or technical education largely for boys, and other large occupational groupings.

While vocational tracking has been influential in the past, it has now mostly disappeared from high schools. Now, in most cases, tracking is likely to be based on assumptions about subsequent education. That is, schools will have a general track for students perceived as not bound for college; a college-bound track; a higher track often called "honors"; and at some schools, an AP (Advanced Placement) track or an IB (International Baccalaureate) track. The names of these may differ from school to school, but the end result is the same: A hierarchy develops which ranks students from the highest levels of performance—as measured by past academic work and likely college attendance—to the lowest level of ability and performance headed for unskilled labor or the surplus pool of available workers.

Sometimes students take all their courses within their own track and sometimes they only take one or two subjects—especially mathematics and science—in separate tracks. Sometimes tracks are reassessed periodically, and sometimes they are relatively permanent. But regardless of these differences, debate has always raged about the ways in which students get assigned to tracks as well as the definition of "ability." The use of test scores and grades may appear to measure ability objectively, but it is not the only way students get assigned to tracks. In many cases, African American and Latino students have been placed in general or vocational tracks based on the assumption that they are not "college material." For the same reason, working-class girls have been assigned to home economics or retail occupation tracks, and working-class boys have been placed in industrial or vocational education. And rather than relying on student or parental choice, tracking assignments have often been engineered by guidance counselors, using biased judgments about who is or is not academically inclined. Under such conditions, vocational and general tracks have come to be seen as "dumping grounds" for students who are not academically well-prepared or college-bound, neglecting the larger question of how tracking assignments are made and whether biased judgments are part of the process.

Many justifications for tracking exist. One of the most common is that it is easier to teach in tracked classrooms because the variation in student abilities—or perhaps student interests—is not as great as in untracked classrooms. Teachers can develop exercises and reading lists that are geared to the middle of the class, without fearing that large numbers of higher- and lower-ability students will complicate teaching. Furthermore, tracked classes allow higher-ability students to move through the curriculum and get to more advanced material faster, while allowing low-ability students to move more slowly and cover lower levels of curriculum materials consistent with their presumed abilities. There is also an argument that students in tracked classrooms will feel more comfortable if they are with students of comparable abilities, whereas they might suffer stigma and lower self-esteem if they are in untracked classes and are thus compared with other students of higher ability levels. But as we will see, issues of stigma show up in several different ways, so we cannot presume that tracking will reduce stigma overall; indeed, it is more likely to create stigma in new forms.

The arguments against tracking are numerous too. Perhaps the most powerful is that tracking places some students in classrooms with fewer resources. Low-track students are likely to have teachers with less experience or training, or those who have been judged as not able teachers; upper-track students are more likely to have experienced teachers with demonstrably strong teaching ability. Low-track students are likely to suffer from their teachers' lower expectations of them, and low expectations generally lead students to expect less of themselves. In lower-track classes, a student's peers are likely to have lower educational ambitions, and because they have been judged to have lower levels of performance or ability, peer effects—the effects of students on each other—will probably affect school performance negatively.

Conversely, in upper-track classes, peer effects are likely to be positive, and encourage students to do their best. Often, upper-track classes have access to advanced mathematics and science labs—less likely to be available to lower-track students. The books and materials available to upper-track classes are likely to be more advanced and richer overall than those in lower-track classes. In other words, lower-track students have access to fewer opportunities than upper-track classes, not necessarily less money, but fewer of the resources that ultimately educate students. (Chapter 5 will explore in greater detail the differences between money and resources.) If we believe that equity means that all students should have the same opportunities and resources, this criticism is a powerful argument that tracking is inequitable.

Another argument against tracking is that students in lower tracks understand that they have been ranked below their peers, and will thus suffer the stigma associated with low performance. Conversely, upper-track students are likely to experience higher status and prestige, which has been confirmed by a large set of ethnographic studies. That is, high-status students—"jocks," or "preps," or "collegiates"—are likely to be in higher tracks while students who are less popular and less engaged with schooling—"burnouts," or "greasers," or "dopers," or Goths—are more likely to be in lower tracks.

What does the evidence about tracking show? The qualitative or ethnographic studies—based on observations in lower-track and upper-track classrooms—document the differential treatment received by students in various tracks. They generally show that students in lower-track classrooms have teachers with less training, less expertise in the field that they are teaching, and fewer resources like labs and books. The curriculum is usually a simplified form of the academic curriculum taught in the higher-track classes, and consists of small bits of information without any context that might help students understand how it applies to other subjects or to life outside the classroom.

In contrast, students in higher-level tracks are likely to have more experienced teachers with greater expertise in the fields they are teaching, as well as books, computers, and curriculum materials that are richer and more advanced. The curriculum content is likely to include higher-level conceptual material—rather than rote memorization and drill—and to explore the possibilities for applying the material to other subjects and problems. In every way, this kind of evidence supports the claims that lower-track classes receive much weaker forms of education than do students in higher-track classrooms, and that the inequalities between the two are substantial and pervasive.

In addition, there is a good deal of quantitative or statistical evidence about tracking, which several commentators have called "the Great Tracking Wars" because the evidence has led to contradictory findings (see Oakes, 2005; versus Loveless, 1999.) The quantitative literature demonstrates that tracking harms lower-track students a great deal, but does not benefit upper-track students much, so that *on average*, homogeneous (from the Latin root for "same") or tracked classes produce greater inequality among students. In these results, "performance" is almost always measured by test scores on standardized tests, which of course are only one measure of educational performance, something we discuss in greater detail in Chapter 6.

The quantitative literature has also asked a different question: whether de-tracking (or un-tracking) is likely to enhance the equity of schooling. This is a complex question because de-tracking requires much more than simply putting students of different ability levels in the same classroom—a change that would probably ensure that lower-performing students continue to do poorly compared to higher-performing students. Instead, analyzing de-tracking requires us to ask what kinds of changes occur when homogeneous classrooms are replaced by more mixed-ability classrooms. Such changes might involve a number of mechanisms for coping with heterogeneous classes: project- or problem-based learning; additional supports for students who initially perform at lower levels; cooperative learning, where students collaborate and learn from one another; instruction that matches classroom teaching to the preparation levels and interests of students; and "multiple pathways," which integrate academic and occupational subjects in a sequence of courses that focus on a broad occupational area like health or communications technology. (On the complexities of de-tracking, see two books, both entitled *Beyond Tracking*, one by Pool and Page, 1995; and the other by Oakes and Saunders, 2008.) But because de-tracking takes so many forms, statistical evidence has sometimes led to contradictory findings.

In some cases, the evidence has revealed increases in average performance and reduction of inequalities among students; in others, the evidence has revealed the precise opposite. Not surprisingly, these empirical findings have led some scholars to argue that tracking is inequitable under all conditions, while others accept the trade-off that preserves tracking and the better performance it brings for higher-ability students. But even though the "tracking wars" have taken place in the pages of research journals, it is a mistake to think that the proponents and opponents of tracking are only researchers. Parents frequently take positions based on where they think their children are likely to be assigned. Dating back to the beginning of the 20th century, battles have erupted between middle-class parents favoring tracking and working-class parents opposing it, in response to proposals for new kinds of tracking (like AP courses) or proposals for de-tracking (replacing homogeneous classrooms with heterogeneous ones, or opening AP courses to all students who want to take them). Teachers also participate in the battles; they are likely to favor de-tracking if they have a high commitment to equity, but otherwise the apparent ease of teaching in tracked classrooms leads teachers to support tracking. "Tracking is one of the most divisive issues we have," said an official of the National Education Association (http://www.edweek.org/ew/issues/tracking/), because it pits teacher against teacher over equity and instruction.

What does all this have to do with racial discrimination? From the origins of tracking in the late 19th century, it has been clear that lower-income students, racial minorities like African Americans and now Latinos, and immigrants are most likely to end up in lower tracks even given other evidence of their abilities. African American and Latino students have often been labeled as "not college material," and therefore assigned to the general high school track rather than to any of the college-bound tracks. So from the standpoint of racial minorities, the existence and persistence of tracking are unambiguously negative: it is all too likely to steer them away from the highest educational opportunities, without providing any benefits.

De-tracking and Re-tracking

As mentioned above, de-tracking has taken many forms, some of which are more thorough and substantial than others. However, it is also possible to have de-tracking followed by re-tracking—that is, efforts to create hetero-geneous classes with students of many ability levels may then generate practices that mimic tracking once again. For example, if teachers working in de-tracked classes group students based on their apparent ability levels, then among-class tracking just gets replaced by within-class tracking, which is sometimes called "ability grouping." Or if classes are de-tracked without providing some kind of additional support to those who initially perform at lower levels, then students will continue to differ in their mastery, and the greater equity associated with de-tracking will not occur. Similarly, if students are allowed to select their own classes and tracks, their choices are likely to replicate older patterns; some will opt for less demanding classes while others—more likely to be middle class and White—elect more demanding, academically oriented tracks.

Even when schools adopt "multiple pathways" as a way of de-tracking, the occupations around which the pathways focus may lead to re-tracking. For example, a school offering pathways in high-status areas like health occupations and in low-status areas like automobile repair will inevitably see re-tracking occur, because only working-class and male students are likely to elect pathways with working-class occupations as their focus. Given the long history of pressure to track and sort students by ability levels, de-tracking is likely to be fragile, and educators concerned about the equity of schooling must watch for signs of re-tracking at every point.

Among-school Tracking

While tracking usually refers to within-school tracking in separate classrooms, it is important to recognize that *among*-school tracking is just as important, if not more so. Among-school tracking takes place when different groups of students attend different schools, again with higher and lower levels of resources like teachers and advanced curricula. Within school districts, this is likely to happen when residential segregation exists; that is, when high-income and low-income families—or Black, White, and Latino families—live in different parts of a city and go to different schools.

At the high school level, some cities have established different types of high school, with vocational high schools, college preparatory high schools, some selective schools with competitive admissions, and others offering the general track that fall somewhere in between. Such cases generate conflict about the admissions process for college-oriented versus general high schools, with opponents and proponents arguing over the conditions for entry. The terms of debate are precisely the same as the argument over how students are selected for high tracks and low tracks *within* schools, except that the differences occur *among* schools.

In response to evidence of residentially based segregation—or tracking within a district—some districts have tried to create policies that ensure that the racial composition of each school reflects the district average. This would avoid some schools becoming predominantly White and Asian American, while others are dominated by Blacks and Latinos. Some of these plans, which are also forms of school desegregation, have worked as intended, but others have been challenged in courts as racially discriminatory. So undoing the kind of segregation or tracking that occurs among schools may be difficult legally as well as politically.

Tracking also occurs among school *districts*, particularly as metropolitan areas develop high-income and low-income communities and as income and racial segregation intensifies. In the United States, a common form of racial segregation exists between central cities and their suburbs, with central cities and inner suburbs predominantly lower-income, African American, and Latino; while outer suburbs are predominantly white and middle class. The causes of racial segregation are many and varied. They include economic segregation, in which only upper-income families can afford housing in certain high-cost communities; zoning, in which some communities place limits on the number of moderate-income housing units; redlining, in which banks refuse to lend in low- and moderate-income neighborhoods; and the location of publicly subsidized housing. But whatever the mechanism for racial and economic segregation, the end result is the separation of different classes and races into different communities.

Then students in these communities attend different schools, obviously. Like within-school tracking, among-school tracking is likely to result in different levels of resources in different communities. For example, suburban schools are more likely to have experienced teachers, whereas urban schools are more likely to have teachers with emergency credentials, less experience, and who are teaching assignments outside the areas of their academic preparation. Unlike their suburban counterparts, urban schools experience a great deal of instability as teachers and students move among schools more frequently. Often the administration in urban districts suffers from high turnover itself, as well as experiencing intense racial and political conflicts over the direction of schools. In many ways that have been examined by qualitative and quantitative research, city schools on average provide fewer opportunities than do schools in middle-class and White communities, replicating the patterns of differences among tracks. (For an accessible account of city versus suburban differences in resources, see Kozol [1991].)

Unfortunately, there are fewer solutions for among-school tracking than there are for within-school tracking. If the problem were just one of selective high schools, then the solution would be to open up these high schools to all students and make sure that every student had been adequately prepared in middle school—something easier said than done. But among-school tracking that is caused by residential segregation can only be addressed by reversing housing segregation, or by busing students from one region of a district to another, as was the case in the 1970s and 1980s. This has been highly controversial and even declared unconstitutional when busing was based on racial criteria. As a result, districts must be careful both politically and legally when they attempt to remedy the kind of tracking that comes from residential segregation.

Solutions are even tougher to find when it comes to tracking among *districts*. Reversing racial segregation among districts requires policies against the long-standing practices that established segregation in the first place, like racial preferences, redlining, and the very location of public housing and schools. While there have been some examples of cross-district busing—for example, from cities to suburbs—they are few and far between. Neither local governments nor courts have been willing to intervene to move students across district boundaries; when such proposals arise, the opposition from parents and teachers is often fierce. The result is that residential segregation leads to among-district tracking with very little hope of reform. The inequities are especially serious when districts differ greatly in spending per pupil and in resources like experienced teachers, ones who teach in their areas of specialization, schools with greater stability, and less turnover of teachers and administrators. In such cases, among-district tracking—like within-school tracking and within-district tracking—leads to differences in the opportunities that children have.

In sum, among-school tracking has many of the same influences as within-school tracking, even though it does not generally get as much attention as within-school tracking. And it is a more difficult problem to correct, particularly when it is caused by residential segregation. In such cases, low-income children of color are likely to be left back in central cities and inner suburbs where they have fewer educational opportunities than their peers in suburban districts.

The Future of Tracking and Choice Mechanisms

The future of tracking is difficult to predict because so many mechanisms support and oppose it. Certainly, most educators' opinions since the first edition of Jeannie Oakes's book *Keeping Track* (1983) have favored de-tracking schools and devising different mechanisms for making de-tracked classes work in more equitable ways. The 1990s, in particular, saw a great deal of action around de-tracking. But currently, the fervor of the earlier de-tracking movement seems to have dissipated. Unless reformers pay close attention to what happens, re-tracking is likely to occur. Furthermore, without opposition to tracking, the status quo will probably prevail. So the future of tracking remains uncertain at best.

An additional uncertainty involves choice mechanisms. Since the mid-1980s, school choice mechanisms—arrangements where parents choose which schools their children attend—have grown substantially. They include charter schools, magnet schools, vouchers, tuition tax credits, inter- and intra-district choice plans, home schooling, and other alternatives. Choice programs have increased the variety of schools available, particularly as small charter schools with varying emphases have started to displace larger conventional public schools that all look about the same. By definition, then, the expansion of choice mechanisms has almost surely increased differences among schools. The question for the future of tracking is whether the proliferation of different schools will increase or decrease the segregation of working-class and racial minority students from middle-class and White students, or whether it will replicate the patterns of ability grouping. Such patterns would concentrate high-ability students in certain choice schools, and low-ability students in other—lower-quality—schools of choice and in the remaining public schools. Under these conditions, choice mechanisms would become other forms of tracking.

On the one hand, a number of charter schools have opted to "specialize" in racial minority students, and their Black and Latino parents have chosen those schools because they think them superior to the neighborhood public schools. Another trend has been the tendency to develop "themed" charter schools, like Afro-centric and Latino-oriented charter schools. By definition these charter schools increase the segregation of racial minority students from White and Asian American students, but they may also be superior schools if they are more supportive and more demanding of their students than are conventional public schools.

A number of state studies have found that charter schools over-represent White and middle-class families while they under-represent Latino working-class families in particular, as well as special education students. Many forms of choice mechanism provide advantages to parents who are "active" choosers, who actively seek out the best alternatives for their children. Evidence from both the United States and Great Britain indicates that "active" choosers are more likely to be middle class and well educated. So there are several mechanisms embedded in the expansion of choice that might lead to the greater segregation of White students on the one hand and racial minority students on the other hand. But if choice schools are superior to the alternatives—something that has not been established so far—then perhaps quality issues trump those of tracking and segregation.

Indeed, the proponents of choice mechanisms argue that choice-oriented schools must improve in order to compete for enrollments, thereby improving the quality of education over that of conventional public schools. If this were true, then the growth of charter and magnet schools might eventually replace low-quality public schools with higher-quality, better-resourced choice schools. Then, if the racial composition of choice schools matched that of public schools, their expansion could lead to similar proportions of White, Black, and Latino students enrolling in choice schools and benefiting from enhanced resources. (As Chapter 5 will clarify, resources may not refer to funding levels as much as the kinds of resources that make a difference to students without costing much money, like levels of trust and cooperation within the school, pedagogical approaches, or richer and more meaningful curricula.)

However, the data on schools created under choice mechanisms suggest that only a few of them are superior to the public schools, a larger number are inferior to the average public schools, and the large number in the middle are not particularly different from the public schools. If this outcome persists, then it would be reasonable to forecast that superior charter schools will be chosen disproportionately by middle-class and White parents; that inferior charter schools will be located in central cities and attended by the children of less active choosers and racial minority students; and that choice mechanisms as a whole will widen the disparities between White students and racial minority students.

Since the mid-1970s, choice mechanisms and choice schools (especially charter schools) have increased, and this trend is likely to continue over the next several decades—though currently, choice schools enroll only about 5 percent of all students. What remains less clear is what the class and racial composition of choice-oriented schools is likely to be. But existing patterns of differences among schools suggest that White parents living in segregated suburban districts are likely to live near choice-oriented schools focusing on White and middle-class students; whereas Latinos and African Americans in central cities will have not only fewer choices, but also be restricted to schools where students of color predominate. If this turns out to be true, then choice mechanisms unambiguously create forces that exacerbate interschool tracking and segregation. The result is that tracking and racial segregation will become more rather than less prominent, without enhancing the quality of schools overall.

Tracking in Postsecondary Education

Tracking is usually considered a problem for elementary–secondary education. However, it also occurs in postsecondary education and has some of the same consequences for educational opportunity. Tracking in postsecondary education is often a direct result of tracking in K–12 education, which means that practices in the latter have long-lasting effects on students' life chances.

The first form of tracking in postsecondary education is the difference in access to colleges and universities. The students who go to college are more likely to be middle- and upper-income students, while low-income students are most likely to end their education with some high school or a high school diploma. This means that the opportunities for postsecondary education are more likely to be closed off for Latino and African American students than for White students. The barriers to enrolling in post-secondary education include income, knowledge of how to apply to college, understanding of financial aid programs and the true costs of college, and lower grades and test scores. All of these factors are part of "college readiness." As a result, in 2008, 72 percent of White high school graduates were attending college, compared to only 56 percent of black graduates, and 64 percent of Latino graduates. To counter these factors, many public and private initiatives across the United States seek to persuade low-income students and students of color about the importance of doing well in high school, and they provide information to students and their parents about admissions procedures, financial aid, and other aspects of applying to college.

Those who do manage to enroll in college encounter further tracking mechanisms. One is that colleges differ substantially in whom they admit and what they offer. At the top of the pyramid are élite research universities and private liberal arts colleges, which are much more likely to accept students of higher income levels. In the middle is a bewildering array of colleges offering Baccalaureate degrees, but differing in terms of their quality, graduation rates, and the kinds of students they admit. Many of these are likely to be regional four-year institutions—state colleges rather than universities—which have much lower admission standards than élite research universities, much lower completion rates, fewer opportunities for postgraduate education, and less access to high-income employment.

Finally, community colleges or two-year colleges are non-selective, meaning that they do not require test scores and grades in order to enroll, and these colleges are where first-generation, working-class, and racial minority students are likely to enroll. But these three types of institution (and in reality, there are many more than three) also provide different levels of resources for students. Élite colleges typically spend the most money per student, and provide a rich array of student support services as well as conventional classes. Their graduation rates are higher than those in other institutions. They are also more likely to lead to postgraduate options, like graduate schools of law, medicine, engineering, and other degrees more advanced than the Baccalaureate. Regional colleges spend somewhat less than research universities and their services are more limited. They often have graduation rates of 45 percent to 55 percent, with some as low as 35 percent. And they are much less likely to prepare students to advance into postgraduate education.

Community colleges generally offer only certificates and Associate degrees. Students who seek the Baccalaureate degree need to transfer to four-year colleges, and the transfer process—like the process of admission to postsecondary education—is itself more likely to leave behind students of color. Community colleges spend much less than regional colleges do; they have fewer student support services; and completion and transfer rates are often quite low, on the order of 20 percent. On the other hand, community colleges have lower tuition levels than other colleges. Because they do not have selective admissions, they are "open admissions" institutions, and are particularly attractive for those lower-income students with middling high school records. As a result, community colleges offer the dominant form of access to postsecondary education among students of color, and many people consider them to be the most equitable kind of postsecondary education. However, like tracking in high schools, the division among these different types of postsecondary institution still leads to different levels of resources for students, including spending levels, student services, graduation rates, and access to further educational opportunities.

Other forms of tracking exist in postsecondary education. The choice of majors is one, particularly since different majors lead to different levels of earnings and employment. For example, science, mathematics, and business majors typically lead to greater earnings than majors in the humanities. The payoffs for attaining professional degrees, like those in health professions and engineering, are particularly high. While there is much more to college than access to well-paid occupations, the fact remains that gaining entrance to some majors provides occupational advantage over others.

Unfortunately for students of color, low mathematics scores in high school often steer them away from majors in the so-called "STEM" fields of science, technology, engineering, and mathematics, which are generally well-paid and which are projected to have shortages in the future. Thus, the selection of majors makes a great deal of difference to subsequent opportunities, this time in employment. In addition, many colleges and universities offer courses for majors and parallel courses for non-majors. For example, the introductory mathematics courses required for mathematics majors are known to be more rigorous than those required for non-majors. Moreover, élite universities have their own version of honors courses, such as the "honors collegium" at the University of California, Los Angeles (UCLA), where students who qualify receive a different kind of experience and curriculum than the average student.

What initiatives and programs seek to minimize the effects of these forms of postsecondary tracking? In terms of access to college, the most prominent—and the most controversial—has been the effort to establish affirmative action by both class and race by giving compensatory admissions to lower-income students and to students of color. However, some observers consider affirmative action itself to be racist because it provides advantages in admissions to African American and Latino students that White and Asian American students typically do not have. So affirmative action has consistently generated controversy, and courts have limited the forms that affirmative action may take. For example, in California, the courts upheld Proposition 209 (1996) which effectively bans affirmative action in college enrollment, causing a drop in Latino and African American enrollment in the University of California system.

Other less controversial programs seek to attract students of color to college—for example, by supporting their work in high schools and providing help in the college admissions process. Still other programs seek to attract students of color and women to STEM fields, by advertising their advantages and by providing special preparation in the basic science and mathematics necessary to major in them. There are literally hundreds if not thousands of such programs across the United States, varying in the specific services they provide, but all seeking to enhance access to—and completion of—postsecondary education for low-income and racial minority students.

But as well-intentioned as these programs are, they vary substantially from region to region in the United States and are often unavailable to students. Also, such programs often rely on support from private funds and therefore tend to vanish when such funding disappears. Finally, these programs vary substantially in their effectiveness; given the prevalence of K–12 tracking, many of the programs provide too few resources too late to make much difference. At best, these are stopgap measures compared to the potential effects of assuring all students adequate preparation in K–12 education to go to college, to make choices among types of colleges, and to decide which majors to choose.

As postsecondary tracking clarifies, tracking begets tracking. Being in a lower track in elementary school will probably lead to lower tracks in middle school, particularly if assignments are based on achievement. Lower-track placement in middle school will then probably lead to lower-track placement in high school. In turn, lower-track students in high school are less likely to gain access to college. If they do, they will most likely find themselves in community colleges, or in the less selective four-year regional colleges. And being in a lower track in high school probably means that their preparation in mathematics and science is inadequate, so they will be less likely to choose high-value STEM majors while in college. Thus, the effects of tracking at one level of schooling will almost certainly be replicated in tracking at subsequent levels, including postsecondary education. This precisely paints the institutional basis of tracking, its oft-cited rigidity—once you are in a particular track, it is difficult to get out—and its effect on students' trajectories. Some of those effects are overt and some of them quite subtle; some are more pronounced in middle and high school, while others are more important in postsecondary education. But all forms of tracking limit the opportunities available to students who find themselves in lower tracks, and these are very likely to be racial minority students.

Positive Pathways and the Dilemma of Difference

When most people complain about tracking, they view it in a negative sense as a practice or program that restricts the opportunities of some group of students—girls/young women, Latinos, or immigrants, for example—who will not have access to forms of schooling with the richest opportunities. However, there are positive forms of differentiation as well, and understanding them is crucial to another definition of "tracking." Good examples of positive pathways are programs for the gifted and talented, open to those students who have performed particularly well. Such programs provide access to smaller classes, more experienced teachers, advanced curricula, more challenging standards, and more rigorous learning opportunities in future schooling and then in college. For students selected into gifted and talented programs, these effects—of greater resources and opportunities—are likely to be positive, so this may be the most obvious form of positive pathway. But, as with forms of negative tracking, access to such positive opportunities is likely to be biased by class and race so that fewer low-income, Latino, and African American students are likely to be included. Some schools have tried to resolve this inequity by opening up gifted and talented programs to all students, and giving those with weaker preparation additional time and support to complete advanced coursework. For the most part, though, positive tracking creates advantages for only some students, just as negative tracking creates disadvantages for others.

Other forms of positive pathways have the same characteristic. Programs and majors in women's studies, African American or Latino studies, for example, provide new opportunities for women or students of color, and few would consider them to be negative forms of tracking. For immigrant students, special programs for English-language acquisition are often viewed as positive opportunities, by helping English Language Learners (ELLs) to learn academic English more quickly than they otherwise would. But some programs of language acquisition are more effective in teaching English than others. For example, strong bilingual education—which uses both English and the native language for instruction—is more effective than other so-called "immersion" programs, which provide very little support to students and which may actually have negative effects. Similarly, for students with disabilities, special education tracks have been developed that do a better job of teaching such students than conventional classrooms can, by modifying instruction so as to overcome the barriers that specific disabilities present to academic achievement. But since special education has not been viewed as particularly effective overall, what might be a positive opportunity again gets converted into negative tracking.

One way to distinguish positive pathways from negative tracking for the same group is to examine the "dilemma of difference" articulated by Martha Minow (1991). When we are faced with two groups of children who differ in some way—for example, ELLs, or children whose native language is not English, compared to native speakers of English—we can choose either to ignore the difference and deem it unimportant, or to pay some attention to it. If we pay attention to the difference and construct special programs for this group, then the children may suffer stigma for being different in some way from "regular" students; but the group may also benefit from enhanced programs that constitute positive pathways through appropriate teaching. If we ignore the difference, then there is no possibility for stigma coming from a special program, but then differences in learning needs will be ignored and ELLs will not receive special support.

Even more dangerously, if we recognize the differences and create *ineffective* English-language acquisition programs, then we run the risk of both stigmatizing students and putting them in negative tracks. But the first decision is whether or not to group ELL students, and there is no choice about doing one or the other. The second decision is whether to assign them to programs that are positive and effective, or to assign them to ineffective programs—negative tracking once again. In short, failing to recognize differences may do harm. But recognizing differences may also do harm, because of the stigma and potential consequences of negative tracking. Only where there are positive opportunities—assignment to programs of greater effectiveness than conventional schooling—can we be sure that identifying differences creates greater benefits for the students selected.

Similarly, for students with disabilities, assignment to special education carries with it an unavoidable stigma, because such students are labeled "different." This stigma may be counter-balanced if the programs to which the students have been assigned are more effective than conventional programs in dealing with their disabilities. A good example of such an effective program is assigning hard-of-hearing students to a class that teaches them lip-reading and signing, which would not happen in the regular curriculum. Once again, the difference between negative tracking and positive opportunities is whether tracking leads to more effective resources or not. If not, then students with disabilities would be better off in regular classes, a process known as mainstreaming.

Similarly, the federal government's major program to aid disadvantaged students—Title I of the Elementary and Secondary Education Act (1965), aimed at low-income students—has been criticized for making little or no difference to the education of low-income students. But that is probably because Title I funds have often been spent on *ineffective* programs—like pulling students out of their regular classes and causing them to miss material that their peers are learning—rather than effective programs; or on providing especially rigid teaching that is limited only to basic skills.

We can now understand what "equitable tracking" or equitable pathways might look like. It would identify groups of low-performing students and then provide them with additional resources—smaller class sizes, more experienced and able teachers, more appropriate teaching approaches, a richer curriculum—in order to improve their education levels. That is ideally the form that most "compensatory" programs aspire to take, whether they are funded by Title I, by foundations, or by private funds. While such compensatory programs separate low-performing students from their peers, they are rarely considered negative forms of tracking. Of course, they may still be ineffective. The current version of Title I, called No Child Left Behind (NCLB), has been challenged as ineffective because its demands for testing and accountability outweigh any additional funding that the programs provide, and because its unintended consequences are largely negative. (Chapter 6 will examine high-stakes testing and accountability programs in more detail.) So everything depends on the effectiveness of the additional resources that might create positive opportunities.

Other debates concern the mechanisms by which individual students are labeled "disabled" or "special ed." Parents generally want such labels when they think the resulting programs will be beneficial, but not if they doubt the programs' effectiveness. Similarly, the loudest debates about Advanced Placement (AP) and International Baccalaureate (IB) programs concern which students will get assigned to these apparently rigorous approaches to the high school curriculum. The evidence shows that AP and IB programs disproportionately enroll middle-class, White, and Asian American students, as positive pathways usually do, while racial minority students are under-represented.

In sum, positive pathways, like negative tracking, have quite a bit to do with race and ethnicity. Some forms of positive pathways, like Advanced Placement programs, suffer under-representation of African American, Latino, and some other racial minority students. Other positive oppor-tunities—like compensatory programs aimed at low-performing students or programs designed to help ELL students learn English more effectively—have over-representation of racial minority students. Unlike negative tracking, which almost universally harms students enrolled in lower tracks, the consequences of supposedly positive pathways depend on the additional resources that are involved. The arguments about positive pathways therefore require us to be even more precise than usual about the resources and opportunities that tracking provide and whether those resources are effective or not.

Segregation, Desegregation, and Re-segregation

Segregation, desegregation, and re-segregation are not usually included when people discuss tracking. However, segregation often works in precisely the same way that tracking does: Some groups of students get assigned to low-resource programs whereas others benefit from greater educational resources. When we ask about the mechanisms that limit the educational opportunities of racial minority students, we should therefore include segregation and desegregation, and recognize their similarities to tracking.

Of course, segregation can take many forms. Boys and girls are often segregated from one another in sex education and physical education classes. Younger students are separated from older students, first by grade, and then in elementary versus middle schools versus high schools. However, the word "segregation" usually applies to racial segregation, initially between White and African American students, and more recently the segregation of Latino students from their White, Black, and Asian American peers. So the term "segregation" has a closer connection to race than tracking does, even if they work in similar ways.

In the years before 1954, segregated schools were common in both the North and the South. The usual justification was the old racist idea that different races should not mix. That idea received legal support from the 1896 case of *Plessy v. Ferguson*, which ruled that segregated facilities could be legal if they were "separate but equal." Although *Plessy* dealt with segregated public transportation, not schools, the courts applied its logic to public schools. As the beginning narrative in Chapter 2 argues, the problem is that segregated school facilities for White and Black students were never equal. Black students attended dilapidated schools, with much larger classes, teachers who had scarcely more education than the students despite their cultural match, and fewer materials of all kinds than White students enjoyed. Like negative tracking, segregation resulted in haves and have-nots, where Black students were always among the have-nots. (We should not exaggerate the racial differences because many White students in poor and rural areas also got limited schooling with inadequate resources just as Blacks did, but their experience was due to poverty and not race.)

The landmark court case in segregation was the 1954 *Brown* decision, in which the Supreme Court finally overturned the notion of "separate but equal." It ruled that the Board of Education of Topeka, Kansas could not continue its *de jure* segregation, which meant legally requiring segregated schools. The *Brown* case specifically rejected the argument that separate facilities could be equal, and pointed to the poor state of schools for Black students as evidence that separate was inherently unequal. The difference in resources—now between White and Black students rather than high and low tracks—was crucial to attacking the inequity of segregation.

Although the *Brown* case eliminated *de jure* segregation within districts, in practice, two kinds of opposition emerged. One was that, given the depth of racist feelings, many Southern districts simply refused to obey the court and continued to require their public schools to remain segregated. Over time, however, the federal government's enforcement of *Brown*, including the use of National Guard troops at Little Rock, Arkansas and the University of Mississippi, broke down this resistance to desegregation, and by the 1960s, even Southern schools looked very different.

The other kind of opposition to the *Brown* case was a more subtle and difficult form of segregation that emerged in Northern and Southern schools alike—*de facto* segregation. *De facto* segregation was not based on policies and laws, but rather on factors that the *Brown* decision could not control. One such factor has been residential location. In the cities of both the North and South, White families—aided by banking practices and public housing policies—moved to the suburbs in order to escape desegregated schools, thereby re-creating segregation. This time, the segregation was *among* districts, just like some forms of negative tracking that we saw earlier in this chapter. In other cases, White families sent their children to private schools in order to avoid desegregated public schools. So the *de jure* segregation that *Brown* found to be unlawful triggered *de facto* re-segregation that was beyond the control of the courts. While desegregation of White and Black students increased until the late 1980s, since then the effects of location and re-segregation have reversed this pattern. Now, White and Black children are increasingly likely to go to different schools, which is why we need an analysis of tracking within schools attended by White and minority students, and among schools and districts where we may find predominantly White- or minority-attended schools.

The case of Latinos and immigrants in general has been somewhat different. In the 1950s, when the *Brown* case was decided, Latinos were still a very small minority in the United States. The most intense conflicts over desegregation involved Black and White students rather than Latino or other racial/ethnic minority students or ELL students. But as the Latino population in the United States grew, it tended to create patterns of segregation where recent immigrants moved into neighborhoods and ethnic enclaves different from those inhabited by Whites and Blacks. The reasons included income differences, since Latinos were unlikely to have enough money to move into middle-class suburbs; cultural preferences, where new immigrants preferred to live in neighborhoods dominated by their peers in order to create language and cultural communities; and other forms of segregation caused by controversial policies like zoning and redlining. Such forms of *de facto* segregation, like the segregation of African American students, isolated Latino students from their White and Black peers, and this form of segregation has increased steadily since the 1950s. (See, for example, Orfield, 2001.)

The result of this *de facto* segregation has been to create richer schools in suburbs and poorer schools in central cities and sometimes inner suburbs—"urban" schools marked by majorities of African American students, and/or recent immigrants including Latinos; high levels of poverty; inexperienced teachers; inadequate facilities and materials; high turnover among students, teachers, and policies; and other negative conditions associated with low-quality city schools. In contrast, suburban schools have been better able to support the positive conditions associated with high academic performance.

In many ways, *de facto* segregation—like among-district tracking—has been hard to attack directly because it is not the result of educational decisions, but rather of housing segregation that determines where families live and send their children to school. Efforts to challenge *de facto* segregation—for example, busing Black students to White suburbs, or changing the boundaries of school districts to create more integrated districts—have always generated fierce resistance. So have efforts to build mixed housing, with some units reserved for moderate-income families while others are priced higher by the market. In short, outlawing *de jure* segregation was difficult and it took many years of litigation culminating in *Brown* and subsequent enforcement efforts. But outlawing or eliminating *de facto* segregation has proved nearly impossible. Despite nearly 60 years of trying to integrate schools, most schools are as segregated as they were in the days of *de jure* segregation. Just as was true in the olden days before the *Brown* decision, *de facto* segregation also reduces the resources available to racial minority schools. And just as schools may experience re-tracking, they may also experience re-segregation, for reasons beyond their control.

There have been some partial solutions to the problem of re-segregation. One is for districts to develop magnet schools, particularly in areas like science and mathematics, that are so attractive that parents of all races want to send their children to such schools. Another related approach has been to develop pathways or forms of "linked learning" that integrate academic and occupational education around some theme, like biology and health professions, economics and business occupations, or science and lab technicians. Under the right conditions, these pathways can also be conduits to postsecondary options, and they therefore become attractive to middle-class students, helping to keep them within the public schools and within the districts that offer them. For inter-district segregation, however, the solutions must depend on housing markets rather than school policies. For example, building integrated housing or re-gentrifying urban neighborhoods can mean that districts—and therefore schools—are racially integrated. But, as has been mentioned before, these policies have had limited success because of resistance from White middle-class parents.

Segregation and desegregation are among the most contentious subjects in all of American social policy. They reflect long-standing fears about racial mixing, and the deepest and most overt forms of racism. It is little wonder that there have been so few solutions to the general problem of school desegregation. It is difficult to ask schools to desegregate when the larger society does not. The upshot is that housing and other forms of social segregation continue to undermine the equity of schools despite decades of effort to fight them.

Do Schools Have to Track and Segregate Students?

The prevalence of tracking and segregation, re-tracking and re-segregation raises the question of whether there is something inherent in schools leading to so much inequitable grouping. Several conceptual formulations have suggested that the answer is yes: that the special roles of schools in our society lead them inexorably to differentiate groups of students from one another. Others have disagreed with these views.

One school of thought is called "structural functionalism." It was popularized by a sociologist named Talcott Parsons (1951), who argued that schools are functional to—or supportive of—society and its many different roles. In our complex modern society, these include gender roles, occupational roles, and roles of citizenship—and schooling prepares students for all of them. But in an unequal society, this means that schools "naturally" prepare individuals for unequal occupational roles reflecting the division of labor under capitalism—some as skilled professionals and others as unskilled labor, for example; or some as active citizens and others as non-participants. Therefore, schools are inherently unequal as they prepare students for adult roles in our unequal society.

A second conceptual formulation reflects a Marxist perspective (see, for example, Bowles & Gintis, 1976). It also maintains that schools are supportive of the larger society, but more particularly, its class divisions between capitalists and workers. Therefore, schools will educate individuals who are likely to become members of the ruling—or professional—classes in different ways from those likely to become routine, unskilled workers. The net result is, again, to segregate students based on class, race, and gender; and to economize on the resources dedicated to working-class and racial minority youth since it would be pointless to spend them on students destined for the working class.

The third conceptual formulation can be called "vocationalist." It notes that schools, colleges, and universities have during the 20th century become much more vocational—or professional—in their goals (see Grubb & Lazeron, 2004). Schools prepare individuals for occupations both overtly—in business courses and business schools, for example; and covertly—in the kinds of high school tracking that then leads to occupational tracking in postsecondary institutions. When preparing students for unequal occupations, a vocationalized schooling system will replicate the inequalities in labor markets, including differences among occupations and the kinds of racial discrimination that we see in employment and earnings.

Other more egalitarian views insist that schools are relatively autonomous from the rest of society, and need not reflect the inequalities there. In the United States, these egalitarian views often depend in some way on the 19th century conception of the "common schools," which included all students and shared a common curriculum. (In reality, the common schools of the 19th century were segregated by race and by class, even though the ideal argued for students of all backgrounds to attend school together.) The common schools sought to provide civic and moral education, so that in a country of equal citizens, their schooling should also be equal. (Again, the reality was different from the rhetoric, since African Americans did not get the vote until after the Civil War and women not until 1920.)

But as civic and moral values weakened over the 20th century, and as occupational goals increased, the pressures for relatively equal schooling systems became weaker and the pressures for occupational sorting grew stronger. Still, concerns about equity have never died out and so we see in schools a constant tension and anxiety over unequal outcomes. Tracking and segregation are good examples, challenged by egalitarian programs like de-tracking, desegregation, compensatory education, and other programs that allocate more resources to students who might otherwise perform poorly.

Therefore the direct answer to the question of whether schools have to track students is no, they need not. Many examples exist of untracked and de-tracked classrooms, which illustrate their potential power. However, at the same time, we need to recognize the powerful forces that lead to tracking and sorting students by their abilities, their potential futures, and sometimes their own interests. So whether equalization triumphs always involves conflict and the outcome is always an empirical issue.

In the end, tracking and segregation pose some of the most enduring issues in schooling. Should schools be differentiated among students? If so, what kinds of differentiation are appropriate, and in which grade levels? Who should get what kinds of educational resources? In a differentiated system of schooling, what distribution of resources is fair or equitable? And if the distribution of resources seems unfair, is that a small price to pay for the advantages of a differentiated system, or are the inequalities associated with differentiation, tracking, and sorting inevitably too great to tolerate in a democratic society? So issues of differentiation and sorting, those of resources, and those of fairness or equity are invariably comingled in discussions of tracking and segregation, and it is no wonder that these remain among the most contentious issues in American education.

Study Questions

1. In the middle and high schools you attended, or in the school where you now work, were there (or are there) *overt* mechanisms of tracking? Ability grouping? Occupational tracking? College-related tracking? Are

there any *covert* forms of tracking; for example, when students in advanced courses take many of their classes together?

2. If there are tracks, how do they differ in the resources provided? Remember that resources refer not necessarily to money, but to those educational inputs that provide students with greater opportunities (see Chapter 5 on the differences between money and resources).

3. Are there groups of students in these schools who receive relatively more resources than other students? Are these programs or classes predominantly comprised of one race, or ethnicity, or class?

4. Are there forms of intra-district or among-school tracking that you can identify? Differences among districts within your region?

5. In the college or university with which you are most familiar, are there mechanisms of tracking? Which of them operate by student choice? Which of them are due to institutional policies; for example, the requirement of high school grades or test scores?

6. What patterns of racial or ethnic segregation have there been in your school or college? You might, for example, compare the proportion of African American or Latino students in particular programs or majors with their representation in the school or community as a whole.

7. As in question 2, are different levels of resources available to students in these different groups?

8. What have been the most contentious battles over tracking and segregation in the schools and colleges with which you are familiar?

Selected Readings

Bowles, S. & Gintis, H. (1976). *Schooling in capitalist America*. New York: Basic Books.

Grubb, W. N. & Lazerson, M. (2004). *The education gospel: The economic power of schooling*. Cambridge, MA: Harvard University Press.

Kozol, J. (1991). *Savage inequalities*. New York: Harper Perennial.

Loveless, T. (1999). *The tracking wars: State reform meets school policy*. Washington, DC: Brookings Institution Press.

Minow, M. (1991). *Making all the difference: Inclusion, exclusion, and American law*. Ithaca, NY: Cornell University Press.

Oakes, J. (2005). *Keeping track*. 2nd Ed. New Haven, CT: Yale University Press.

Oakes, J. & Saunders, M. (Eds.) (2008). *Beyond tracking: Multiple pathways to college, career and civic participation*. Cambridge, MA: Harvard Education Press.

Orfield, G. (2001). *Schools more separate: Consequences of a decade of resegregation*. Retrieved May 13, 2013 from http://civilrightsproject.ucla.edu/research/k-12-education/integration-and-diversity/schools-more-separate-consequences-of-a-decade-of-resegregation/orfield-schools-more-separate-2001.pdf.

Orfield, G., with Schley, S., Glass, D., & Reardon, S. (1993). *The growth of segregation in American schools: Changing patterns of separation and poverty since 1968*. Cambridge, MA: Harvard Project on School Desegregation.

Parsons, T. (1951). *The social system*. New York: The Free Press.

Pool, H. & Page, J. A. (Eds.) (1995). *Beyond tracking: Finding success in inclusive schools*. Bloomington, IN: Phi Delta Kappa Educational Foundation.

Funding, Resources, and Racism

When Money Matters

In 2007/2008, Americans spent US$10,440 per student in public kindergarten through to 12th grades, for a total of US$600 billion. At first glance, this seems like a great deal of money, though it pales in comparison to the amounts for other kinds of public spending: defense (US$687 billion), health (US$2.6 trillion), and social welfare (US$1.5 trillion). So whether overall spending on education is too large—as anti-tax advocates claim— or too small—as parents and schooling advocates often assert— depends on the kinds of comparisons we make.

Still, the amount spent on education, particularly public schooling, is highly visible because it represents a major portion of state and local government spending. Of total state government spending in the United States, 26 percent is for public K–12 education and an additional 13 percent is for public postsecondary education. The comparable figure for local education spending is 39 percent, almost all of which supports K–12 education. This virtually guarantees that school budgets are carefully scrutinized by every state and local government. Ever since the mid-19th century, advocates supporting higher spending for public education have had to fight tax cutters who opposed taxation and funding for schools. Horace Mann—often considered the father of public education—declared that such opposition to taxation was "embezzlement and pillage from children," and similarly strident rhetoric has continued ever since. These battles are particularly fierce during times and in places where enrollments are growing. Therefore, the impulse to expand education as the solution to every conceivable problem, including that of equity, has always run up against resistance to public spending.

One consequence of these battles is what we call the Money Myth. This is the notion that *funding* is the central problem in education, that improvements require additional funding, and that school reform and greater effectiveness cannot happen without additional funding. A prominent educator named Elwood Cubberley expressed these sentiments as early as 1905, when he wrote: "One of the most important administrative problems of today is how properly to finance the school system of a state, as the question of sufficient revenue lies back of almost every other [educational] problem." (For these and other quotes, see Grubb, 2009, Chapter 1.) The same sentiments operate in present-day concerns about school finance, school budgets, the taxes that support schools, and other dimensions of funding.

However, as we will see in subsequent sections, the Money Myth is not always right. Indeed, it is difficult to find any consistent relationship between spending per pupil and student outcomes, and it is easy to find expensive programs that have no effect whatsoever on students. Such findings have led to extensive debate about whether money matters to outcomes or—more precisely—about the conditions under which money *might* matter. And doubts about the effects of funding make it necessary to find an alternative to the Money Myth. For us, the alternative focuses on the *resources* or inputs that go into schooling—like teachers, instructional approaches, materials, the culture of schools, the expectations of students, and many other kinds of inputs, only some of which can be readily purchased. Such a shift from funding to resources also helps explain why the Money Myth is incomplete and sometimes wrong.

Regardless of the focus—whether it is money or resources—*equity* is a central question in the support of schools, particularly the differences among students in different regions. Such differences, or inequalities, have been pervasive and take many forms, only some of which are racial. But the different levels of funding and resources in schooling have been so pervasive that it is always worth asking whether they have exacerbated or lessened the differences among students of different racial and class groupings.

The Patterns of School Spending

One of the greatest concerns among those who study school spending has been the equity of funding. An obvious kind of inequality exists among states, based on the amount they spend per pupil. For example, the highest-spending state in 2008/2009 was Wyoming, at US$18,068 per pupil, and the lowest-spending state was Utah at US$7,217 per pupil. (These spending levels have been adjusted to consider cost differences among the states.) Some variation among states is due to simple income differences; that is, certain low-spending states like Mississippi and Alabama simply have lower tax bases from which to raise school revenues. However, states also *choose* to spend higher or lower amounts on schooling. For example, California (a relatively wealthy state) restricts property tax revenues—thereby restricting school expenditures; whereas Massachusetts opts to increase the rate at which it taxes itself for schools.

Moderating the differences among states would require some kind of federal effort—for example, directing federal funds so that low-income states could raise their average levels of spending. However, currently the federal government provides only 9 percent of total revenue for schools, almost all of which goes to programs for high-need students like those in low-income families, those who are English Language Learners, and those in special education. There never has been much interest in expanding federal funding to equalize expenditure differences among states, so such variation is likely to persist.

Moreover, inter-state differences are likely to matter more and more in the coming years. Schooling for K–12 is moving in the direction of a national curriculum, and 46 states have already adopted Common Core academic standards that have been developed for the United States as a whole, covering English and mathematics in grades K–12. When tests are developed in line with the Common Core State Standards, we will probably see more comparisons among states—particularly since the assessments being developed seek to ensure such comparability. Some disparities will be due to different expenditure levels, and without any federal mechanism to reduce such disparities, variations in outcomes will also persist—to the detriment of students living in low-spending states like Mississippi and California. All of this will become increasingly obvious, and might generate pressure to alleviate inter-state differences in funding.

Of the many types of inequality in school funding, funding *among* school districts within states has received the most attention. In almost every state, it is possible to find districts that spend four to five times as much as other districts. Advocates for equity have spent a great deal of energy to identify and remedy these inequalities. In general, local revenues for schooling depend heavily on the property tax, so that wealthy school districts—with high-value residential property associated with high-income residents, as well as commercial and industrial property—can afford to spend much more for schooling than property-poor districts can. To combat these funding differences, proponents of equity have pressed for state revenue formulas that direct more state revenue to poor school districts than to wealthy districts. The variety and complexity of such funding formulas have become overwhelming—labeled by some as "the minutiae of educational equity." Despite these legislative efforts, the magnitude of inter-district inequalities remains substantial in almost all states.

In their efforts to establish more equal funding across districts, proponents of equity have often turned to the courts. Ever since the *Serrano v. Priest* decision in 1973 found California's school funding system unconstitutional, lawyers in virtually every state have tried to use state or federal constitutions to challenge inequality in school funding. While these lawsuits have generated great enthusiasm among advocates for equity, their effects on resources for students—as distinct from the symbolic effect of highlighting inequality—remain doubtful. In many states, the lawsuits have not overturned the current structure of funding; in others, the legislative response has been too weak to change the patterns of funding. In still other cases, patterns of funding have changed, but have not led to any greater *resources* in poor school districts. And even when resources have been equalized, outcomes like test scores and graduation rates have not become more equal. The result is that differences remain high in both inputs and outcomes among districts within states, despite the variety of efforts to reduce them through legislation and litigation.

In addition, there are often funding differences among schools *within* districts. This usually happens when teachers with seniority are able to choose the schools in which they teach. This concentrates higher-cost, experienced teachers in schools with predominantly White and middle-class students, while relegating inexperienced, low-cost teachers—many of them on emergency credentials—to other schools within a district, those more likely to have racial minority and low-income students. This pattern occurs frequently in large urban districts with many schools.

Some districts have tried to solve this particular form of inequality by allocating funds to schools based on weighted pupil formulas. Typically, weights are higher for low-income students, for English Language Learners, and for special education students; for example, a low-income student might have a weight of 1.10, generating 10 percent more revenue than other students with weights of 1.00. Schools with higher proportions of these high-need students therefore receive more funding than other schools. (In some districts, weights are higher for different levels of schooling, like the high school compared to elementary school students, or for students in expensive programs like vocational education or gifted and talented programs.) The use of weighted formulas is a way to eliminate the inequalities due to teacher allocation and also to redirect more funding to schools with more high-need students (or more expensive programs). So far, however, only a handful of districts have adopted weighted pupil formulas, though there is considerable interest at both the local and state level in the use of such formulas.

Another subject of considerable interest in school finance is the difference between central-city versus suburban districts, because high-need students tend to be concentrated in central-city schools with poor educational conditions. (See, for example, Jonathan Kozol's *Savage Inequalities* [1991] for a description of the conditions in city schools versus their suburban counterparts.) In fact, however, city schools and suburban schools do not differ so much in their levels of funding, because many central cities have substantial tax bases from commercial and industrial property. Rather, central-city and suburban districts differ in the resources they can provide for their students, as *Savage Inequalities* eloquently showed. Jacob (2007) has demonstrated that average city district spending in 2003/2004 was US$7,812—slightly *higher* than average suburban district spending of US$7,542. (Spending in all schools that year averaged US$7,268.) However, the higher levels of spending by city districts did not lead to higher levels of *resources*: Central-city schools had higher numbers of students per teacher (15.0 versus 14.6), lower teacher salaries (US$45,400 versus US$46,100), a higher proportion of schools with temporary buildings (37.3 percent versus 34.4 percent), and a higher proportion of schools using common spaces for instruction (21.3 percent versus 19 percent). Thus, funding levels do not tell the whole story of what really goes on in schools. To understand the disadvantages of urban schools, where the majority of African American and Latino students are enrolled, we must shift our focus beyond funding by itself and look instead to the *resources* that are provided.

Although legislation and litigation about inequality have devoted great attention to spending differences, in many ways the focus on funding has been inappropriate and inadequate. Since the origin of the Money Myth in the mid-19th century, times have changed. The challenge facing public schooling is no longer to provide classrooms, teachers, and toilets. Instead we ask for more powerful learning (or at least, higher test scores), fewer drop-outs, a reduction in achievement gaps—improved *outcomes* rather than simple *access*. If these are the goals, it is difficult to show that spending more money leads to superior outcomes (Hanushek, 1989). Real, inflation-adjusted spending per pupil has risen substantially, from US$685 in 1919/1920 to US$6,663 in 1982/1983 (when *A Nation at Risk* was published and started the current movement for school reform) to US$11,470 in 2004/2005—without improving preparation for adult life or reducing inequalities in outcomes, or solving any of the other education problems at the heart of school reform. Many district, state, and federal "reforms" have come and gone, with billions spent and little to show for them. Contrary to Cubberley, we cannot spend our way out of educational problems.

We need a new approach, in place of our fixation on revenues and expenditures, and on finance formulas as mechanisms of reform. After all, dollar bills do not educate children. Teachers with particular instructional approaches, principals capable of instructional leadership, schools with supportive climates, and many other resources do. A better approach, presented in Grubb (2009), embraces an explicit concept of *how* money affects outcomes, by increasing or (all too often) failing to increase the specific *resources* that affect outcomes. It broadens the conception of school resources, recognizing differences among simple, compound, complex, and abstract resources. It rests on a statistical analysis of the richest data set we have, the National Education Longitudinal Study of 1988 (NELS:88), to show that other myths—especially that school resources do not make much difference—are wrong. Finally, it suggests several steps for enhancing the capacity of districts and schools to develop more effective resources.

When Money Does Matter

In several direct and indirect ways, money does matter to outcomes. Modern schools are not the informal places of the 18th century, and they demand teachers, administrators, materials, and increasingly elaborate facilities. These all require money, especially as we integrate special education students, create programs for English Language Learners, install computers and multi-media centers, and provide other resources unknown even two decades ago. But such spending provides only *access* to schooling, not necessarily enhanced *outcomes*.

A few effective resources, improving learning or progress through school or student attitudes and values, do require additional spending. Based on statistical results (in Grubb, 2009), teacher salaries improve outcomes, because they allow districts to attract a larger pool of applicants from which they can choose the ones judged to be the best qualified. Higher salaries also reduce teacher turnover—one of the negative influences on outcomes. The adult–pupil ratio—not a measure of class size like the teacher–pupil ratio, but a measure of personalization—also affects progress through high school. Teacher experience in secondary education enhances several outcomes, and so does access to counselors; both require greater funding, of course. In these cases, *simple* resources—where spending per pupil leads directly to the resources it buys—make a difference. Put another way, when a simple resource is effective *and* requires money in obvious ways, then money makes a difference to outcomes.

In a less direct way, personalizing high schools enhances progress and completion. Schools are more welcoming when they have more adults and counselors, closer contacts in advisory relationships, other adult relationships in internships and service learning, and better working relationships with teachers in theme-based approaches. But these all cost money in obvious ways.

Finally, some negative consequences of low spending affect other hard-to-measure dimensions of education. In many states, including California, cuts have imposed more duties on teachers and administrators. Many schools cannot improve because their teachers and leaders have no more time and energy, and have become weary of "reforming again, again, and again." This consequence emerges only over time, and cannot be readily detected in conventional statistical analysis. But simply hoping to remake schools into "lighthouse" or effective schools cannot work if there is no time or energy for reform. In effect, time and energy are resources that depend on funding, though in these cases, the influence of money is complex and indirect rather than simple and direct.

What Undermines the Effects of Money

While money affects outcomes in several ways, many examples of increased spending do not change outcomes, and some even make them *worse*:

Money Is Wasted

Money can be embezzled, or spent to hire friends and relations. More often it is spent on ineffective resources—incompetent teachers, or weak after-school programs, or teacher aides without clear plans. Money may be spent without changing practices; a good example is using ineffective professional development—like Friday afternoon one-shot workshops—to try to make complex changes like improving instruction. Money is often spent piece-meal, buying whatever the restricted grants of a government or a foundation require without an overall plan, or spending year-end money wildly. Legislatures often fail to pass budgets early enough to allow districts and schools to plan for the school year. All too often, principals and other school leaders know little about the funds they control and about using resources effectively. Perhaps worst of all, money gets spent on potential long-run benefits, like improving the school climate or changing instruction—only to have a new principal or a superintendent with different priorities reverse course, and then those earlier resources go to waste.

The conditions for waste seem more serious in urban districts because of sharper political disagreements, racial and ethnic conflicts, different approaches to reform, the challenges of educating students from low-income families, and the instability caused by mobile students, teacher turnover, principals coming and going, and new superintendents. Thus, not only do many urban districts lack additional revenues for high-need students, but they also seem more likely to misspend the monies they do have.

Some Ineffective Programs Cost More Money

Some expensive practices actually *reduce* test scores or progress through high school. Key statistical results show that this is most obvious for traditional vocational education (which costs more than academic programs), the "general" track, and the remedial track dominated by drill and practice on basic skills. Such tracks are what we call *compound resources* with multiple elements: less demanding teachers, watered-down curricula, unmotivated peers, and lower expectations for college. Special education represents another program with high spending but minimal effects on conventional outcomes; while U.S. society prefers inclusion rather than exclusion of special education students, such equity goals have negative effects on the relation between spending and outcomes. High-cost continuation schools and alternative education for low-achieving students have similar problems, as do "compensatory" programs for low-income students. Finally, some spending looks "ineffective" because its goals are not measured by conventional outcomes; for example, spending on campus security, especially high in urban districts, seeks to keep students safe, but has no effect on test scores or graduation rates.

Urban districts spend a great deal of money on second-chance efforts: alternative education, remediation for low-performing students and those who have failed exit exams, and various other interventions. These practices intend to support low-income and racial minority students through their schooling. They reflect a commitment to equity and to the responsibility of schools (rather than families alone) for academic performance, but they operate under difficult circumstances. Students who have experienced earlier failure or mistreatment may be reluctant to intensify their schooling. Peer effects work in counterproductive ways since second-chance programs concentrate on low-performing students. Such programs are often asked to make several years of gains in one year or less, yet there is little evidence about which programs work. Spending money on second-chance programs may be a justifiable and equitable response to under-performing students, but it weakens the relationship between money and outcomes.

Many Reforms Fail to Understand that Compound rather than Simple Resources Are Necessary

Class size reduction provides a clear case of a compound resource. For example, the billions of dollars that California spent on class size reduction were—on the average—ineffective because districts hired lower-quality teachers, funded inadequate professional development to facilitate different instructional methods, and provided insufficient space. Other examples of ineffective resources include new curricula, approaches to assessment, and computers because all of them require professional development in addition—itself a complex resource. (Effective professional development requires sustained attention to pedagogical issues by a faculty working collaboratively.) When districts or states provide money for simple resources, the money is often wasted unless it can be combined with complementary resources. Put another way, money is often necessary, but not sufficient.

Many Effective Resources Cannot Be Bought

For example, there is no store that sells improved instruction. According to key statistical results, reported in Grubb (2009), several complex and abstract resources affect test scores or progress through high school, including:

- teachers' use of time;

- departmental encouragement of innovation;

- teachers' control over their own classrooms;

- innovative or "balanced" pedagogy, especially in mathematics;

- a positive school climate;

- negative events like drug dealing and fighting;

- low school-wide rates of attendance, measuring overall student commitment.

Complex resources, like approaches to instruction, are themselves complex as well as difficult to change. Abstract resources refer to dimensions of schooling, like trust and school climate, that are themselves quite abstract.

In addition to the statistical results, studies have documented the effectiveness of two other abstract resources: curricular coherence, and trust (Bryk & Schneider, 2002). Higher spending per student does not increase these resources. Instead, teachers and leaders working together must *construct* them by developing school-wide approaches. Money may be necessary for ancillary purposes—release time for teachers, occasional outside experts, literacy or mathematics coaches. But money is less important than vision, principal leadership, the cooperation rather than the resistance of teachers.

The need to *construct* certain resources shows why conventional school finance strategies—like equalizing spending per student, or litigation to force more equitable spending—do not guarantee effective schools. The emphasis on allocating money and simple resources usually ignores compound, complex, and abstract resources whose money costs are often indeterminate, and which depend on other resources that cannot be bought.

Closing Achievement Gaps Cannot Be Done with Money Alone

Current demands for reform often focus on achievement gaps, which are almost always stated in racial terms like the differences among White, Black, and Latino test scores, or the drop-out rates of Latinos compared to White and Asian American students. Conventional policy then recommends improvements in teachers, smaller classes, or intensification like after-school classes. However, many policy recommendations ignore the glaring fact that these "gaps" are related to race and ethnicity.

The best statistical data available show that profound differences among African American, Latino, and American Indian students on the one hand and White and Asian American students on the other *cannot* be explained by variables describing family background (or class), unequal school resources, or students' commitment to schooling. Those variables fail to explain between 45 percent and 61 percent of the Black–White differences in test scores; 25 percent to 40 percent of White–Latino differences; 45 percent of the Black–White difference in earning a high school diploma; and 20 percent of the White–Latino difference. Put another way, racial/ethnic inequality remains, even after controlling for every conceivable variable, in the richest data we have.

Anyone who is serious about eliminating achievement gaps has to explain these differences, and then come up with solutions. One powerful hypothesis is that many students are mistreated—sometimes based on class differences, but most often based on race and ethnicity. Substantial testimony comes from African American and Latino writers remembering their own schooling; from ethnographers describing particular schools; from critical race theory and its personal stories; and from our own observations in schools and community colleges. Mistreatment can sometimes be overt and conscious as in the physical abuse of students, but more often consists of covert and unconscious "micro-aggressions" that are individually small but collectively relentless insults to students. Racial minority students are less likely to find adults who can serve as mentors and sponsors; they are more likely to be the victims of lower teacher expectations; and they are more likely to be suspended or expelled for infractions for which other students are not punished. These practices start early: The trajectory of school practices that set racial minority students up for failure begins as early as 4th grade.

To combat these forms of mistreatment head on, advocates have developed many strategies—in effect, a range of complex and abstract resources. These include finding more teachers of color; explicit attention to code-switching (shifting from one kind of language to another) for immigrant students and speakers of Black Vernacular English; culturally relevant pedagogy and multicultural education that bring new curriculum materials; new subjects (like the role of race in American society) and new pedagogies with more critical perspectives; systematic classroom observation so that teachers can learn if they are unconsciously mistreating students of color; different approaches to discipline; non-teaching support from same-race counselors and mentors. (The previous chapters have discussed some of these issues.) All of these are examples of complex and abstract resources, which must be constructed by teachers and leaders working together within specific schools. Sometimes money is necessary for outside experts, facilitators of difficult racial conversations, release time, or curriculum materials. But other abstract resources are more important; they include clear diagnoses, vision, cooperation, persistence, and above all, trust (Bryk & Schneider, 2002). Once again, money is necessary, but not sufficient.

The Shift to Resources and Equity Effects

By now it should be clear that it is not sufficient to focus only on money and funding in education. Instead, we need to pay attention to the resources that money can buy. Throughout this chapter, we have referred to four categories of resources—simple, compound, complex, and abstract—to show that inputs to schools go far beyond the simple resources that dominate the Money Myth and to understand how money is actually spent. The categories of complex and abstract resources remind us of the importance of school characteristics like trust; coherence; the stability of students, teachers, and administrators; approaches to instruction; and school climate. These and other dimensions of schools are not only relatively abstract, but also cannot be bought in any straightforward way. They rarely show up in any analysis of school finance because their connection to funding is so weak and unpredictable. But they should remind us of how wide the conception of resources can and should be.

Once we recognize how broad the conception of resources can be, it is straightforward to carry out a "resource audit," parallel to the fiscal audit that conventionally takes place in school districts. A resource audit starts with a list of potential educational resources, and then asks whether a particular school has them or not, and how they might be put in place (Grubb & Tredway, 2011, Tool 3-C). Such an audit can serve to remind schools of the complex and abstract resources that they may lack, but that they might implement with relatively little funding.

In addition, a shift away from money and toward resources helps explain why the relationship between money and outcomes is so weak. As we argued in the previous section, it helps us show that some money is wasted and some resources—especially those that are complex and abstract—cannot be bought, so in general, only simple resources follow the pattern of money buying more of a resource that enhances outcomes. Focusing on resources also helps to show specifically how funding can be ineffective: For example, the category of compound resources illustrates that several simple resources may be jointly necessary to make a difference, and omitting any one of them undermines the overall effects of spending.

Most importantly, focusing on resources rather than money helps us to understand the inequities in schools. It turns out that although expenditures per pupil are unequally distributed, as various lawsuits illustrate, many other resources are much more unequally distributed than are expenditures. For example, among simple resources, the pupil–teacher ratio is distributed particularly unequally, as is the certification of teachers. Among compound resources, teacher experience, planning time, and staff development are distributed less equally than money. In high schools, the tracking mechanisms discussed in Chapter 4—especially placement in general, vocational, or remedial tracks—have particularly negative effects on all kinds of outcomes for students. Such mechanisms can be considered powerful kinds of compound resource since they reflect differences in teacher and student aspirations, in the quality and rigor of the curriculum, and in peer effects. Among complex resources, the use of teacher time and innovative teaching are much more unequally distributed than is spending per student. Among abstract resources, certain dimensions of school climate are also highly unequal, and a book like *Savage Inequalities* (Kozol, 1991) has illustrated many types of inequalities between urban and suburban schools that concern *resources*, but not necessarily funding. These inequalities are the ones we have already highlighted as adversely affecting racial minority students: being in schools with inexperienced teachers; with teachers teaching out of their field of expertise; with high turnover rates among teachers, administrators, and students; with a lack of trust and supportive personal relationships; and—as we argued above—with varieties of mistreatment of African American, Latino, and sometimes low-income students. These inequalities—of resources, not funding—help explain the racial achievement gaps in schooling, while a simple focus on funding does not.

So the Money Myth is true some of the time, and no one should ever be allowed to claim that money makes no difference to the outcomes of schooling. But the Money Myth is limited in various ways, and shifting from a focus on funding to an analysis of resources provides much greater insight. It also clarifies that while African American, Latino, and immigrant students are sometimes the victims of unequal funding, they are more powerfully the casualties of unequal resources.

Building the Capacity to Make Resources Matter

We have seen that while money sometimes leads to enhanced outcomes, its effects are just as often either zero or negative. On average, the relationship between spending and outcomes is close to zero. Doing something about this conundrum is particularly urgent now, when most states have seen their tax revenues plummet and when available funding seems woefully inadequate.

Recently, several researchers and educators have addressed this problem, in articles with titles or subtitles like "What money can't buy," "Using resources effectively in education," and "Solving the funding–achievement puzzle." Most call for reductions in waste. For example, some commentators excoriated the waste of classroom time, the difficulty of firing obviously incompetent teachers, ineffective professional development, and most remediation. Others critiqued the waste of time on ineffective instructional practices like worksheets and movies, and exhorted educators to replace them with purposeful lessons and coherent curricula. Layoffs based on seniority (rather than teaching ability) may be other examples of waste, along with paying more to teachers with Master's degrees. Some critics have suggested new forms of professional development, reallocating resources from specialists to regular classroom instruction, replacing remediation with prevention, and enhancing efficiency—again, reducing waste. Of course, every school and district ought to undertake an audit of waste, which is quite an easy exercise (Grubb & Tredway, 2011, Tool 3-A). But eliminating waste collides with the interest groups, union rules, and bureaucratic mechanisms that created waste in the first place. And eliminating waste does not tell anyone what to do instead.

A second tactic is to increase the incentives for schools and districts to spend resources well. Eric Hanushek and Alfred Lindseth (2009) called for clearer standards and accountability, and for rewarding performance at every level from teachers' and administrators' pay to state funding formulas. Their program assumes that schools do not have adequate incentives to improve. But this seems quite wrong: Every school we have visited knows its scores on state and federal accountability measures, and every high school feels pressure to increase graduation rates. Schools do not need more incentives to do well, but rather the capacity to respond to the incentives they already have.

So the commentary tells us what not to do—waste resources—but it says nothing about what resources to invest in, or how to create a system where schools and districts have the capacity to allocate and construct resources more wisely. This requires at least four transformations:

1. Carrying out routine "waste audits," especially at the school and district levels, to see where funds are being misspent. Similarly, a "resource audit" (in place of a fiscal audit) can clarify which of the many *effective* resources have been developed within a school, and which are missing.

2. Decentralizing decision making about resources to the school level, and adopting school-based budgeting so that principals and school-site councils have the fiscal resources to develop and implement their own

improvement plans. (Weighted student formulas are clear examples of school-based budgeting.) Currently, districts make most funding allocations, and schools have neither the incentives nor the funds to develop their own resource plans. However, school-based budgeting creates the opportunity and the funding for principals and school councils to develop the resources that are effective at *their* schools, with *their* students and *their* teachers. Along the way, school leaders necessarily become more knowledgeable about "where the money goes," or which resources are enhanced, since they are the ones allocating and developing these resources. School-based budgeting with weighted student formulas also has the potential of being more equitable than the current distribution of spending among schools.

3. Professional development to make school leaders and teachers more sophisticated about *effective* resources. Many existing school-based budgeting systems do not provide professional development that is adequate to enable schools to make better decisions, and this deficiency must be remedied. Furthermore, wise resource allocation requires not only fiscal resources, but other abstract resources as well—leadership, vision, trust, teacher participation, and cooperation. Only the careful development of leaders and teachers can provide these.

4. A What Works Institute that provides user-friendly information about effective (and ineffective) resources to schools and districts. All schools and districts need access to such information for reform, but a school-based system of resource development makes such information all the more urgent. The current federal What Works Clearinghouse is pretty much a failure. It includes only a narrow range of random-assignment and statistically sophisticated studies, ignoring a wider range of evidence. It reports individual studies, rather than synthesizing results across topics of interest to schools (like the use of time, or after-school programs, or 9th-grade remediation). Its results are accessible only to researchers, not to busy principals and members of school-site councils who lack research expertise. Finally, it has been accused of political bias. A better alternative is a network of What Works Institutes, perhaps established at the state or regional level and modeled on the Agriculture Extension Service, which could synthesize research on topics suggested by districts, schools, and state policy makers, and then present the results in research briefs

and conferences. Such institutes would bridge the divide between research and practice, something that would benefit both researchers and practitioners.

These reforms would enhance the fiscal and abstract resources for improving resource allocation, improve the incentives to do so, and provide the expertise necessary for thinking in different ways about money, resources, and effective practices. Without such changes, schools will continue to bumble along, epitomizing the Money Myth, continuing to waste resources without understanding precisely when money matters and when it does not.

For racial minority students, particularly in urban districts, equalizing resources (rather than just funding) would overcome many of the problems faced by urban schools: inexperienced and uncredentialed teachers, turnover of all kinds, a lack of trust, chaotic conditions, insufficient attention to remediation and other interventions for students who fall behind, and so forth. Enhancing these resources would give low-income, African American, Latino, and immigrant students far better chances for equitable schooling than they now have.

Study Questions

1. In the *state* in which you live, look up your state's adjusted spending level per student in *Education Week Quality Counts* indicators (http://www.ed week.org/go/qc12). Is yours a relatively high-spending or low-spending state? How does its relative ranking affect the resources it provides for schools, or the nature of debates over funding in your state?

2. In your state, are data readily available on the spending per pupil in different districts? Which are the high- and the low-spending districts? What accounts for these differences?

3. Have there been legislative efforts in your state to equalize spending per student across districts? Has there been litigation to accomplish the same goals? How effective has each of these strategies been?

4. In your district: Has there been any analysis of high-spending versus low-spending *schools*? Alternatively, has there been any analysis of which schools have the most experienced (and expensive) teachers?

5. Have any districts in your state shifted to weighted student formulas for allocating funding to individual schools?

6. In the school with which you are familiar: What kinds of *expenditures* appear to be wasted? Which *resources* appear to be wasted? For an approach to waste audits, see Grubb & Tredway, 2011, Tool 3-A.

7. Think about the simple, compound, complex, and abstract resources in your school, trying to be as comprehensive as possible. (The resource audit in Grubb & Tredway, 2011, Tool 3-A, may be helpful here.) Which of these require substantial funding? Small amounts of funding? No additional funding, but other resources such as leadership, co-operation, trust, vision, and the like?

Selected Readings

Bryk, A. & Schneider, B. (2002). *Trust in schools: A core resource for improvement.* New York: Russell Sage Foundation.

Grubb, W. N. (2009). *The money myth: School resources, outcomes, and equity.* New York: Russell Sage Foundation.

Grubb, W. N. & Tredway, L. (2011). *Leading from the inside out: Expanded roles for teachers in the schools we need.* Boulder, CO: Paradigm Press.

Hanushek, E. (1989). The impact of differential expenditures on school performance. *Educational Researcher, 18,* 45–62.

Hanushek, E. & Lindseth, A. (2009). *Schoolhouses, courthouses, and statehouses: Solving the funding–achievement puzzle in America's public schools.* Princeton, NJ: Princeton University Press.

Jacob, B. (2007). The challenges of staffing urban schools with effective teachers. *The Future of Children, 17*(1), 129–153.

Kozol, J. (1991). *Savage inequalities.* New York: Harper Perennial.

High-Stakes Testing, Accountability, and Racism

Testing is one of the most familiar aspects of schooling, taking place at all levels from the earliest grades through postsecondary education. Whether a test has low stakes or consequences—like a 4th-grade spelling test; or whether it has high stakes—as do the Scholastic Aptitude Tests (SAT) and American College Tests (ACT) that help determine admissions to college—tests and more complex assessments (like essays and portfolios) have become part of the familiar vocabulary of schooling, for reasons we shall explore subsequently. But testing is more complex than it seems, and the use of tests for high-stakes outcomes inevitably involves debate and controversy. If tests are embedded in accountability systems, with positive and negative consequences for high and low test scores, then they become even more powerful and more controversial—as illustrated by the level of contentiousness over the federal No Child Left Behind legislation. So although the creation of tests may seem simple, in fact there are a number of technical, conceptual, political, and equity judgments made whenever tests are used, all of which influence race relations.

As with everything in schooling, questions of equity and fairness—and therefore the potential for racist treatment—arise in the case of tests and their incorporation into accountability systems. Indeed, by their very nature, tests measure the differences among individuals and therefore are designed to reflect inequality among students. Some of these inequalities may reflect characteristics we want to measure, like the mastery of academic standards, but others may be artifacts of testing and accountability themselves. So clarifying what tests do and do not accomplish under different conditions is a crucial aspect of examining the equity or inequity that tests create, including the impact on racial minority and low-income students. We argue that tests and accountability systems not only reflect inequalities in education, but also serve to create them.

In this chapter, we first examine the origins of testing in schools, since testing has always been associated with measurement and efficiency. We then explore why tests became increasingly common during the 20th century by clarifying the many roles that tests perform. The second section contrasts the apparent simplicity of testing with the actual complexity of creating tests and assessments, to clarify the point that supposedly "scientific" tests require more than most observers understand. In particular, the ways that tests are used often mistake their characteristics and lead to unintended effects. In the third section, we look at the rise of test-based accountability systems—that is, the systems of rewards and punishments attached to tests and assessments. Although accountability is now almost synonymous with No Child Left Behind (NCLB), its origins pre-date this legislation and show up in many different ways. At the same time, NCLB clearly illustrates how accountability systems can go right and wrong, so we take time to explain how NCLB works and what its consequences have been.

In the fourth section, we discuss the implications for teachers of applying high-stakes tests. In the fifth section, we take up the issues of equity and accountability systems. We first ask whether (or under what conditions) tests are fair, and then similarly ask whether accountability measures are fair. In particular, we argue that neither testing nor accountability systems can be fair unless students have equitable opportunities to learn—or put another way, unless school systems have the capacity to respond to tests and accountability. This analysis brings us back to the issue of effective resources that we encountered in Chapter 5: There, we concluded that unless resources are equitable, opportunities to learn will be inequitable and unfair. Similarly, tests and accountability systems are unfair unless resources and opportunities to learn are equitable. So it turns out to be impossible to disentangle the issue of resources and effectiveness from the issue of testing and accountability. Here is where another dimension of racial difference creeps in: Low-income and racial minority students are more likely to suffer from under-resourced schools, influencing the validity of tests and accountability as well as other outcomes.

In the final section, we ask what the future of testing and accountability is likely to be. Just as testing has increased throughout the 20th century, and accountability has grown since the mid-1980s, it is likely that testing and accountability will become more pervasive in the coming years. In particular, the development of national standards and assessments creates new possibilities for accountability, possibilities that might either stimulate learning among all students or might contribute further to inequality. So there are many reasons to be concerned about the future of accountability, and many specific issues for advocates of equity and racial minority students to understand and then to influence.

The Origins of Testing in Schools

Testing has been associated with efficiency for as long as tests have been used in schooling. Tests were used in the 19th century to understand what subjects teachers needed to emphasize, but they received their real impetus from the efficiency movement that blossomed after 1900. This movement, whose business applications were often called "Taylorism," emphasized counting inputs to production in minute detail, as well as outcomes and (in business) profits. Schools began to mimic Taylorism in every way they could, including the measurement of inputs and outputs as if schools followed a factory model of production with raw materials (uneducated students) transformed into finished products (students with greater knowledge) through a production process. The school of thought known as "Social Efficiency" emerged as a way to apply the principles of Taylorism to schools. That was a way not only to process knowledge and information, as Chapter 1 suggests, but also a way to process students.

The field of educational administration was born, obsessed with counting in every way and eliminating waste wherever possible. (Note the analysis of waste in schooling in Chapter 5 on resources.) In this process, tests were obvious ways of measuring the outcomes—the "bottom line" of schools—just as corporations had their bottom line of profit.

In addition, the period after 1900 was a time of differentiating schools by creating tracking mechanisms—initially vocational tracking, followed by ability grouping—and tests were supposedly "scientific" ways of assigning students of different abilities to different tracks. (See Chapter 4 on tracking and segregation.) From the very beginning, therefore, tests were used not only for low-stakes purposes like grading children, but also for high-stakes purposes like allocating them to different tracks and deciding which ones should be held back. Often, given the influx of immigrants to the United

States, the students most affected by testing were immigrant children, relegated to lower tracks by the supposedly scientific use of testing.

Tests became increasingly common during the 20th century. One reason is that tests promise to do so much at relatively little cost (Linn, 2008); they can, among other things:

- help clarify expectations for teaching and learning;

- monitor the educational progress of schools and students;

- monitor the progress of demographic subgroups of students and the gaps in achievement of those subgroups;

- encourage the closing of the gaps in the performance among different racial/ethnic subgroups and between economically disadvantaged students and their more affluent peers;

- motivate greater effort on the part of students, teachers, and school administrators;

- contribute to the evaluation of educational programs and schools;

- identify schools and programs that need to be improved; and

- provide a basis for the distribution of rewards and sanctions to schools and students.

For policy makers, tests and other assessments have promised to give some control over the classroom, while other mechanisms of control—like teacher preparation, professional development, and inspection systems in which external inspectors examine what happens within classrooms—are expensive, complex, and uncertain in their effects. Of course, assessments can also be expensive, particularly if they seek to measure performance in various activities, include open-ended questions, and require answers in the form of essays or portfolios. But the use of tests seems to be a direct, simple, and efficient way of not only monitoring learning, but also directing it.

In short, by the end of the 20th century, tests and other assessments were used for a variety of high-stakes outcomes. Some were the basis of placement; for example, in special education, honors programs, or tracks that depend on measures of ability. Other tests were the basis of admission to college as well as postgraduate institutions like medical schools and law schools. States in the 1980s and 1990s experimented with a variety of test-based accountability systems, often developing standards as the basis for testing, monitoring adherence to those standards, and starting to hold individual schools responsible for meeting the standards. About half the states began to require exit exams before high school seniors could graduate, an apparent effort to increase the standards for graduation. Most of these high-stakes tests had obvious consequences for *students*, but some state accountability systems also had consequences for *schools*. High-stakes testing had become an unavoidable part of the education system at virtually all levels.

The Complexity of Testing

Part of the attractiveness of testing is its apparent simplicity and low cost. Educators and test makers create batteries of questions covering whatever academic content students are supposed to have learned, and the results then reflect the extent of learning from student to student. However, as testing has been elaborated over the last century, it has become an increasingly complex and sophisticated endeavor. To be accurate and useful, tests need to meet a number of conditions.

First, the content of tests needs to be based on precisely defined *standards*, usually referred to as academic content standards. If this is not true—for example, if 4th-grade mathematics tests or 9th-grade English tests are based on different conceptions of what students should have learned in those subjects and grades—the tests will reflect different standards rather than different levels of mastering academic content. As a result, the 1980s and 1990s, a period of increased test making, saw many states setting academic content standards as the basis for testing outputs rather than the inputs of curriculum and resources (see Chapters 1 and 5). Standards themselves are controversial, particularly in subjects like English and history where interpretation is crucial and where little agreement exists about curriculum content. But without agreement from policy makers and teachers on the underlying standards for assessment, tests become relatively meaningless as they do not allow for a constructive comparison of student abilities among schools.

Second, tests need to be *valid*—that is, they should measure what they are intended to measure, rather than something else. For example, mathematics problems sometimes depend on reading ability rather than mathematical competence; reading tests may actually measure background knowledge rather than anything that happens in English instruction. Establishing validity is itself a complex and many-sided challenge, but if tests are not valid measures of what they purport to measure, then their results cannot mean what they seem to.

Third, tests need to be *reliable*; that is, small differences in the administration or scoring of tests should not make a great deal of difference to the outcomes. If tests are unreliable—for example, if there is a great deal of error from one administration of the test to another—then they are not accurate and cannot be used to rank students or to place them in different programs or settings. Like validity, reliability has many different meanings, some quite technical, but an unreliable test (like an invalid test) is close to meaningless and even dangerous for some purposes, because it may misclassify students.

A fourth characteristic of sound tests is the *absence of bias*. Contrary to popular opinion, a test is not biased simply because one group scores higher than another group on a test. For example, the fact that boys generally score higher than girls on mathematics tests does not necessarily mean that the test is biased against girls; instead, it may mean that boys are more consistently encouraged in mathematics and related subjects like computers and science. The way statisticians can tell if the test is biased or not is to use a procedure called "differential item functioning" (DIF), which asks if a subgroup has much higher or lower scores on a particular item (or question) than would be expected from their answers to other items. Unfortunately, while some high-stakes tests like the SAT are routinely subjected to DIF analysis, many others are not. This means that they may be biased against some group, whether based on gender, race, income, or other characteristics.

A fifth characteristic of valid tests is the provision for *accommodating* certain groups for whom testing conditions are especially inappropriate— like students with disabilities and English Language Learners. The development of accommodations is a technically complex and controversial subject, but without such measures, tests are likely to be biased against many Latino and Asian American students.

One of the most important uses of tests has come to be the *comparison of test scores over time*, in order to see whether students have increased their mastery of academic content. But for tests to be valid measures of improvements in learning, they must be constructed so that one point on a test administered at the beginning of the period means the same thing as one point at the end of that period. This result can be accomplished through statistical methods known as "test equating," which is itself highly technical and subject to debate. But the main idea is that tests cannot be used to make comparisons over time unless careful steps have been taken to make them valid for such uses.

In the same way, tests cannot be used to compare two students unless the same test is used. For example, under NCLB, states based their tests on different academic content standards. This makes it impossible to compare the students in Mississippi with those in Connecticut. Such a comparison can be made only if students in these two states (and other states as well) are tested with the same instrument, based on the same content standards. Currently, there is only one test—the National Assessment of Educational Process (NAEP), also commonly referred to as "the nation's report card"— that allows valid comparisons among states.

Another criterion of good practice in assessment is to use *multiple measures*, rather than relying on a single test to make decisions. The use of multiple measures means that errors in one assessment may be offset by errors in another; it also allows for more dimensions of performance to be captured. Unfortunately, the advice to use multiple measures is widely ignored, particularly in cases of high-stakes tests like the SAT (usually reported as a single composite score) or high school exit exams. Furthermore, in many state accountability systems, the only measures that count are tests of state academic standards. This again undermines the possibilities for using multiple measures, such as including grades as well as test scores, for example.

The *equity or fairness* in testing presents yet another issue. There are multiple conceptions of equity, some of which are widely accepted and some of which are controversial. One uncontroversial conception is that tests should be unbiased. Another is that tests should be administered in the same way for all students, so that the scores reflect real abilities rather than the conditions of test taking. (Different test-taking conditions might trigger Claude Steele's (2010) "stereotype threat" or fear of performing badly, causing some students—especially racial minority students sensitive to stereotypes of poor performance—to do less well because of test anxiety.)

A third and more controversial conception of equity is that all students taking a test should have had the same opportunity to learn as others. For example, if one student has teachers who are inexperienced, lack credentials, and face large classrooms of underprepared students, while another student has experienced and highly credentialed teachers with a broad portfolio of teaching techniques and small class sizes, then any test would be an unfair representation of their abilities to master subject-matter content. Instead, the test might more accurately be viewed as a measure of the resources available to the two students, rather than of their knowledge of content. This criterion for testing can also be viewed as an issue of *test validity*, because in this situation the test is not a valid measure of mastery as intended, but rather one of the resources that are available to each student. (Note that this condition for fairness returns to the question of equitable resources, the subject of Chapter 5.)

A particularly controversial conception of equity (Grubb, 2009) holds that test scores should be the same for all subgroups of students—males and females, individuals of different racial backgrounds, individuals of different socio-economic status, etc. Otherwise, some difference in the tests, their administration, or the opportunities to learn should explain differences in subgroup test scores. However, this relatively extreme conception of equity essentially says that all subgroups should score the same on tests that are fair; it does not allow for the possibility that some groups know more than others at a particular point in time.

Finally, for some kinds of tests—particularly those used to rank students, or to provide or deny them access to particular programs—fairness may require provisions for re-taking the test. Perhaps the clearest example involves high school exit exams, where most systems allow students to re-take the exam after a period of remediation—which the school should provide. Students can re-take the SAT/ACT tests, for example, but not end-of-course exams or tests for direction into special education. Particularly if tests are unreliable—so that the results vary from one administration to another—the option to re-take them may be crucial not only to the tests' validity, but also to their fairness.

In sum, there are many ways in which tests can be poorly constructed, misused, or unfair. Therefore, an initial question when facing the complexity of testing is how good any particular test is. If a test is invalid or unreliable, or if an assessment uses only a single test score rather than multiple measures, or a test is unfair because of the students' differing opportunities to learn, then the implications of test scores are not straight-forward by any means.

Another critical question about testing is why it should improve learning: What is it about *measuring* learning that might lead to *improvement* in learning? This question relates to the "theory of action" underlying testing, or the conception of why it might improve the quality of teaching and learning. To answer this question, one must undertake a multi-step process in which each step is crucial before the theory of action can be valid. For a particular test to improve learning, all of the following must be true:

1. The test must be valid, reliable, and unbiased.

2. The teacher and/or school leaders must be able to interpret test scores correctly, understanding what the scores say about the strengths and weaknesses of students and potentially of teachers.

3. Teachers and leaders must have some incentive to improve test scores. This may only be the desire to prevent a poor reputation from having students with low test scores. But if teachers and leaders are indifferent to test scores, then there will be no reason for them to worry about improving them.

4. Teachers and leaders, jointly and individually, know how to improve learning—that is, they understand the changes in instruction, curricu-lum, and school climate that will lead to better learning and higher test scores. This notion assumes that there may be ways of enhancing test scores without improving learning—for example, cheating or "teaching to the test." The emphasis here should be on enhancing the learning that tests are supposed to reflect, not on simply increasing the scores.

5. Teachers and leaders can put these changes in place without interference from districts, unions, parents, state or federal policy makers, resource constraints, or any other potential barriers to changing practices in schools in appropriate ways.

If any of these conditions are not met, then there is no reason to think that testing by itself will make any difference to learning. In particular, point number 4 raises the question of whether schools have the *capacity* to make changes leading to enhanced learning; and number 5 asks whether there are *barriers* to putting these conditions in place. A school that lacks the capacity to make appropriate changes or faces multiple barriers to doing so will be unable to move from information on test scores to improvements in learning. Note that among the potential barriers to change are resource constraints, so once again we need to look at inequities in resources (see Chapter 5) to understand why schools may not be able to respond appropriately to test scores.

So far, the assumptions underlying testing and its theory of action depend on the abilities of educators to react appropriately to the information provided by test scores. But another dimension of tests is that they may motivate *students* to do better, as they come to understand that their own interests are better served by learning more and performing better on the tests. For example, one theory underlying high school exit exams is that students are so motivated to graduate from high school that they will work harder to learn whatever is necessary to pass the exit exam.

Unfortunately, this raises the opposite possibility—the potential for discouragement from low performance. If students perform badly on standardized tests, then they may suffer some kind of stigma and may be further discouraged in their school work. An elegant way of stating this hypothesis is Claude Steele's (2010) theory of "stereotype threat." The social landscape includes stereotypes of many different kinds—that men are better at mathematics than women, that African American and Latino students do poorly in cognitive tests, and so on. Steele has found that when people are reminded of these stereotypes—when the stereotypes are triggered by some event—then they perform worse than they do in a neutral situation. The presence of testing is an example of such a trigger, something that may remind students of the stereotypes of who does well and badly on academic performance assessments. Especially when students' racial identities are involved, such as tests asking them to report their ethnicity or race, they are likely to perform worse on the tests. Perversely then, the very presence of testing may cause some students to perform poorly instead of providing them with incentives to do better in their school work. For example, the best estimate is that high school exit exams have *lowered* high school graduation by about two percentage points instead of improving high school completion—an effect that outweighs whatever positive effects there may be (National Research Council of the National Academies, 2011, pp. 4–5).

Rather than enhancing motivation, then, testing—especially the widespread testing that schools now endure—has the potential to reduce motivation and undermine the self-worth of some students. This reminds us of W. E. B. Du Bois' (1989/1904) incisive question about African Americans: "What does it feel like to be a problem?" In test after test, low-income, Black, Latino, and recent immigrant students score worse than middle-class and White (and often Asian American) students, and the tests reveal racial and ethnic gaps that appear to be relatively fixed. But repeating this finding over and over, while failing to improve the schools that racial minorities attend can only undermine those students' morale and attachment to schooling—especially when the possibilities of stereotype threat are considered. In other words, the prevalence of testing in a world of unequal outcomes has its own negative effects, as well as other unintended consequences that this chapter will address.

So now we face a quandary: Testing is a procedure that is common, popular with educators and policy makers, and increasingly widespread over the 20th century. But there are serious technical difficulties with tests and marked possibilities for inequity and unfairness. These problems are only exacerbated when tests are used as part of accountability systems. For the moment we will leave the potential solutions to this quandary for the concluding section of this chapter, but the contrast between the popularity of tests and their many difficulties should remain front and center.

The Rise of Test-based Accountability

Accountability describes any system that attaches stakes—positive rewards or negative sanctions—to various outcomes. In test-based accountability, the outcomes are, of course, scores on tests and other assessments. Thus an accountability system might give a reward of additional funding to schools with high test scores; or conversely, might threaten schools that have low test scores with having to close or "reconstitute" themselves by replacing teachers and/or leaders. In theory, accountability systems could have a balanced mix of rewards and sanctions; but in practice, rewards have been much less common than negative consequences for low performance, giving accountability systems a kind of punitive sensibility.

Accountability systems can hold *schools* or *districts* accountable for performance; in other cases, they may hold *teachers* and/or *leaders* responsible for performance. Some of them fall on *students* themselves, as the high school exit exams that prevent students from graduating do in the first instance. But then schools with low graduation rates are likely to be forced to provide remediation for students who fail, so that in the second instance, schools may be held accountable for low graduation rates. It is necessary to distinguish carefully what entity is responsible under any accountability system because—as with testing itself—the ability to respond to accountability systems may vary among schools and districts, or among teachers, leaders, and students.

Accountability systems first developed in the 1980s and 1990s, after the 1983 publication of *A Nation at Risk* and the beginning of the current wave of school reform. *A Nation at Risk* included a great deal of economic and military language criticizing U.S. schools for allowing the country to fall behind its international competitors and reinforcing the sense that schools ought to behave more like businesses, as Taylorism and Social Efficiency have encouraged. Accountability systems in education therefore took on many characteristics typical of business, like generating benefits and costs for the "bottom line" of test scores. States in the 1980s and 1990s began to develop their own academic content standards, created tests based on these standards, and then imposed various rewards and sanctions for scores on the tests. Such accountability systems varied greatly, however, making it difficult to compare the results across states.

In 2001, all this changed with the reauthorization of the Elementary and Secondary Education Act, called No Child Left Behind (NCLB). The NCLB Act shifted accountability from a state system to a federal system. It has required all states receiving federal funding to test students in grades 3 through to 8, and once while students are in high school, using state standards and state tests to do so. States must also develop measures of proficiency, and measure all students against those proficiency standards. Furthermore, data are collected for many subgroups of students including those who are low-income, African American, Latino, Native American, Asian American, those who have disabilities or speak limited English, in the hope that information about proficiency will compel schools to be more concerned about low-scoring groups of students than they were previously. (Of course, this assumes that the theory of action underlying testing is valid, which may not be true—particularly if schools lack the capacity to respond.) For the first time, schools provided racially disaggregated data on student performance, which led to support from racial groups who hoped that data on achievement gaps would lead to their improvement. This aspect of NCLB seems to have been quite successful: Schools have paid much more attention to low-performing students under NCLB, because they now face consequences for the way those students are educated.

Another goal of NCLB has been proficiency for all students by 2013/2014. As many commentators have noted, this standard is highly unrealistic, particularly when applied to groups like special education students and those whose primary language is not English. (Recently, many states have gained waivers from this particular requirement.) As part of this goal, states have been required to come up with measures of "Adequate Yearly Progress" (AYP) toward the goal of proficiency, and all students in every subgroup must have an attendance rate of 95 percent or better. Here is where the negative consequences of NCLB begin: Schools which fail to achieve their Adequate Yearly Progress targets for two years in a row are called "Program Improvement" schools, and their students then have the right to transfer to any other school in the district. After three years of failing to make AYP, schools must provide students with supplementary services like tutoring, and may be required by their districts to accept technical assistance including programmatic or personnel restructuring. This commonly involves either converting the school to a charter school, or firing many of the teachers and principals and hiring new ones—based on the assumption that the characteristics of teachers and leaders make crucial differences to outcomes and that better teachers and leaders can be found to replace existing ones. While NCLB involved some positive rewards in the early years, they were never very transparent and they disappeared after a few years. So, like many of the state accountability systems of the 1980s and 1990s, NCLB has a decidedly punitive air, and in particular, blames teachers and leaders for low performance. But as we saw in previous chapters, student achievement is also a function of larger processes, like the division of labor and inequalities among families, over which teachers and administrators have little control. The unintended consequences of NCLB, therefore, include blaming students of color and their families for failing to meet expectations. In addition, NCLB's severe under-funding exerted pressure on struggling schools without providing the resources necessary to help them succeed.

No Child Left Behind is a useful illustration of an accountability system, not only because it is the most important one the United States has now, but also because it shows how complex an accountability system can be. In addition, unlike state systems of standards-based testing, which improve learning only under the theory of action outlined in the previous section, NCLB's accountability provisions try to force enhancement of test scores by imposing punitive measures on schools that fail to improve over time. We might ask, as we did for testing itself, why should accountability work? That is, what is the theory of action, or conception of causality, underlying any accountability system? Again, as for testing, a number of assumptions are necessary for accountability systems to lead to enhanced learning:

1. The underlying tests must be valid, reliable, and unbiased if they are to accurately reflect learning. As before, teachers and leaders need to be able to interpret tests if they are to make progress in improving them.

2. The incentives and punishments under the accountability system must be transparent, and structured so that schools can actually improve their performance by deliberate actions.

3. Schools must have the capacity to see what actions they can take to improve student performance—that is, they must know how to improve learning. In particular, accountability must be able to change what teachers do in the classroom.

4. Schools need to enhance learning rather than just test scores; thus, for example, cheating on tests and narrowly "teaching to the tests" may enhance test scores, but they are not legitimate ways of improving learning.

5. There should be no barriers to schools taking actions to improve student performance—neither resource-related barriers nor political barriers raised by other stakeholders. The political will to address inequality forthrightly must be present.

6. The overall costs of the accountability system—both in money and in terms of other resources—must be bearable. Otherwise those responsible for responding to incentives will be unable to do so. For example, while NCLB has provided additional funding to districts, a common criticism is that the amount of funding is not enough to cover the costs of testing, never mind the costs of responding to the law's mandates. For this reason, NCLB has often been considered a large "unfunded mandate" imposed by the federal government on schools and districts.

7. If *schools* are to be held accountable for student performance, including gaps among subgroups (like male–female differences, or White–African American differences), the schools must be able to control all the factors that lead to test score differences. But of course this is not true: Enormous differences by race, ethnicity, and class emerge in virtually every study. These differences are linked to parental income and education, access to health care, housing, community conditions, and other non-school factors beyond the control of educators. As long as this is the case, then schools will vary according to non-school differences, and under accountability systems like NCLB, schools with low socio-economic status and racial minority students will be penalized relative to middle-class and White schools. These are precisely the kinds of differences that educators have no capacity to improve, since they have no control over the income, health, housing, and other life conditions that contribute to non-school influences.

Evidently, any accountability system will have its desired effect only under special conditions that are unlikely to be met in the real world. Instead of promoting learning, any accountability system in education may have other consequences, unforeseen or unintended.

There is by now a substantial literature on the effects of NCLB, many of which are negative rather than positive:

- Because NCLB relies on tests of reading and mathematics, it has tended to narrow the curriculum to these subjects, and neglect subjects like science, history, foreign languages, and other electives. This narrowing of the curriculum makes it impossible for some students to take courses and earn credits in the wider variety of subjects required for college entrance, so NCLB may enhance reading and mathematics scores at the expense of admissibility to college.

- Because most state tests examine students on basic skills rather than more advanced competencies, state standards encourage repetitive drilling on some skills rather than more conceptual approaches to teaching. This is contrary to the view that students of the 21st century need "21st-century skills" or deeper forms of learning if they are to succeed in a complex and competitive world.

- No Child Left Behind has encouraged several illegitimate ways of enhancing test scores. Stories of cheating by school personnel have become relatively common. More widespread has been the tendency to spend a great deal of the school year on drills related to test questions and preparing students in specific ways to take the test— "teaching to the test," in other words—rather than enhancing learning in more general ways.

• Because NCLB emphasizes proficiency on tests of reading and mathematics, schools have focused more on students on the cusp of proficiency—also known as "bubble kids" since they are "on the bubble" or edge of proficiency—and neglecting high-scoring students who will be proficient no matter what, and low-scoring students with little chance of achieving proficiency.

• Under a system emphasizing proficiency, states have every incentive to lower their standards as a way of increasing the proportion of students considered proficient. Among other things, this means that comparisons among states are not valid because they conflate varying state standards and student performance.

• Schools with high proportions of low-performing students—who tend to be those suffering from inadequacies in non-school conditions like income, health care, housing, and community conditions—have been designated "low-performing *schools*," rather than schools with students affected by inequitable *non-school* conditions. In other words, differences in school performance are ascribed to education rather than to the systematic non-school inequities in an inequitable country.

Furthermore, these unintended consequences have been the most powerful for schools with low-performing students—especially urban schools with high proportions of low-income, African American and Latino students, recent immigrants, and English Language Learners. For these populations, school has become an arid process of test preparation, endless drill on low-level skills, and narrow teaching in only English and mathematics. Rather than improving the education of low-performing students, NCLB has further impoverished their schooling.

In many ways, then, NCLB has backfired and actually reduced serious attention to the conditions of learning among low-performing students, rather than enhancing it. As a report on incentives and test-based accountability in education concluded:

Test-based incentive programs, as designed and implemented in the programs that have been carefully studied, have not increased student achievement enough to bring the United States close to the levels of the highest achieving countries. When evaluated using relevant low stakes tests, which are less likely to be inflated by the incentives themselves, the overall effects on achievement tend to be small and are effectively zero for a number of programs.

(National Research Council of the National Academies, 2011, p. 4)

In other words, test-based accountability systems in general—and not just NCLB—have failed to achieve the effects on learning that they intended. Given the costs associated with accountability systems—the narrowing of the curriculum, the incentive to focus on "bubble kids," the incentives to "teach to the test," as well as the financial costs of testing—one might legitimately ask whether accountability systems are worth the effort. When we examine equity effects later in this chapter, that question will arise even more powerfully.

Applying High-Stakes Tests to Teachers

Some high-stakes tests (like exit exams) hold *students* accountable, while others (those used in NCLB) hold *schools* accountable. But a recent movement uses the NCLB tests to hold *teachers* accountable, in the form of so-called value-added measures.

As with many aspects of testing, the notion underlying value-added measures is simple and appealing. The "value added" of any educational process is a student's increase in test scores over a period of time, like a school year. Then teachers can be held responsible for value added, since their instruction is presumably what causes increases in student test scores. Current proposals include using value-added measures to determine teacher salaries and to make hiring and firing decisions.

But right away, a number of conceptual and practical difficulties arise with value-added measures. Most tests used in NCLB are not vertically equated, so their use in comparing test scores over time is not valid. Many other technical problems arise, especially when test scores are measured with error. Assigning groups of students to teachers is straightforward in elementary school, though even there student turnover makes it difficult to assign some students to individual teachers. But in middle school and high school, where students have multiple teachers, it is hard to know which ones should be responsible for a particular student's reading or writing ability. And many teachers—of language, history, and science, for example—cannot be rated according to value-added measures if the only tests administered are on reading and mathematics. In practice, then, value-added measures can be accurately applied only to a small subset of teachers.

In addition, and contrary to widespread belief, value-added measures do not eliminate the effects of family background, so value added is likely to be higher for middle-class, White students than for lower-income and racial minority students. Moreover, value-added measures cannot possibly eliminate the differences in school capacity—including teacher qualifications as well as more abstract aspects of a school like its climate and general approach to instruction. In short, using value-added measures holds teachers accountable for conditions over which they have no control.

As a result, teachers and their unions have seriously resisted value-added measures. The issue, as Bella Rosenberg (2008) has argued, is not that teachers are hostile to the content standards underlying statewide tests; rather, they object to being blamed for school and district conditions and test variations for which they cannot be held responsible.

How might all of this affect schooling? The conditions that make value-added measures inaccurate are likely to be most serious in underperforming urban schools, where instability, lack of capacity, and low socio-economic status of students are most prevalent. So, low pay, teacher turnover, and insecurity from the use of value-added measures are likely to be most pronounced in precisely those schools that need a stable, confident teaching force. Once more, the use of high-stakes testing that is intended to improve the quality of teaching is likely to backfire—undermining the teaching conditions in schools attended by low-income and racial minority students.

Equity and Accountability

Just as we asked whether tests are equitable and fair, we can ask whether accountability mechanisms are fair. Evidently, the first requirement for test-based accountability to be fair is that the tests themselves be unbiased, and the conditions of test administration equitable. Then if the opportunity to learn varies—for example, because of resource differences—the tests will be unfair and the accountability system resting on these tests will be unfair. As we argued in the previous section, this conclusion suggests once again that resource differences undermine the fairness of accountability systems.

One crucial assumption in the theory of action of accountability systems is that all schools should have the capacity to understand what might improve learning. But if some schools lack this capacity, while others possess it, then the accountability system will again be unfair. Under NCLB, some schools—underperforming urban schools, with high proportions of low-income and racial minority students—have lacked the capacity to improve learning because their teachers have low levels of experience, their leaders and teachers turn over constantly, and chaotic conditions prevail. Those schools also lack the resource of *internal* accountability—the accountability of all members of a school community to one another—which is necessary for responding to *external* accountability measures. The result is that many schools in program improvement have been unable to exit this status because they lack the capacity to improve.

In addition, the accountability measures of NCLB have fallen on only a subset of schools. High-performing schools—like suburban schools with largely White and middle-class student bodies, which get no federal aid for disadvantaged children— have been left alone while low-performing urban schools have been overly scrutinized. As a practical matter, this means that urban schools have become places where students are endlessly drilled on basic English, mathematics, and test preparation, to the detriment of other subjects. That is an impoverished education by any criteria. Thus, an accountability system designed, among other things, to narrow achievement gaps has contributed to a widening inequality among different kinds of schools, with a harsh impact on low-income and racial minority students.

It turns out, then, that the equity requirements in *both* testing and accountability are quite stringent. Specifically, tests have to have the right properties, of validity, reliability, freedom from bias, and so on. Accountability systems need to be transparent and well understood by all participants. Above all, we have to make sure that the capacity to respond to test-based accountability is relatively equal across schools, districts, and states. This brings us back to the question of whether schools have the requisite breadth of effective resources and whether mechanisms exist to equalize those resources. Otherwise testing and accountability serve to create inequalities for low-income and racial minority students, rather than lifting low-performing schools and students to "proficiency," however measured. If NCLB had been accompanied by the money and other resources necessary for these approaches to work well, then it might have succeeded in its goals of improving the learning of low-performing students and narrowing various achievement gaps. But since NCLB imposed accountability without enhancing the capacity to meet its demands, its provisions undermine its laudable goals—making the law high on threats, but low on resources.

The Future of Testing and Accountability

We have already argued that testing is here to stay because of its apparent advantages in education. The same is surely true for accountability, since it is a policy instrument that seems effective compared to the more complex processes of intervening in classrooms. A great deal of commentary has called accountability "a work in progress" or an "experiment," implying that we will see continued efforts to improve it.

Indeed, the likely future of testing and accountability is already apparent. The Common Core State Standards in English and mathematics have been adopted by 46 states, and they will surely influence instruction as these states modify their curricula to conform to the standards. In addition, two large consortia have obtained federal funding to develop tests associated with the Common Core, and one emphasis in these tests will be the ability to make comparisons among states as well as among schools. The Common Core State Standards are therefore likely to be the closest thing the United States has to a *national* set of academic standards; the tests associated with them will be something like a national testing system because they will be used to rank all students, schools, districts, and states.

One can imagine that the next version of the Elementary and Secondary Education Act might use Common Core State Standards as its basis of accountability, which would eliminate one of the most cited flaws in the current system: the tendency for states to vary substantially in the rigor of their state standards. The development of a national accountability system would reveal differences in capacity not only within states—from district to district, or from suburban to rural to urban districts, for example—but also differences in capacity from state to state. Such differences, particularly from low-resource states like California and Mississippi to high-resource states like Connecticut and New York, would further complicate the fairness of accountability by adding an *interstate* dimension to the *intrastate* dimension that now exists. (See Chapter 5 on the kinds of resource inequalities that arise among schools.) So given the development of the Common Core State Standards, we can foresee that the problems with accountability will only grow more serious as certain state education systems fail to perform as well as others.

If we have to accept testing and accountability, we should at least ensure that they are done correctly. The theories of action underlying testing and accountability provide us with criteria that can be used to judge their effectiveness and equity. To sum up, tests must be constructed to be reliable, valid, and fair, and also must adhere to the other criteria for accurate and equitable testing. Accountability systems need to be transparent and well understood by all participants, as well as resting on tests that are accurate and appropriate. Above all, we have to be sure that the capacity to respond to test-based accountability is equitably distributed so that schools have effective resources, and that mechanisms exist to equalize such resources—steps that are not currently part of the Common Core State Standards. Otherwise, testing and accountability simply become mechanisms for creating racial and income-related inequality rather than enhancing effectiveness and equity in schools.

Study Questions

1. In your state, what tests have been used in schools both for state purposes and for No Child Left Behind? What criticisms have been leveled against these tests?

2. Aside from the tests used for state and federal accountability purposes, are there other high-stakes tests in your state—for example, high school exit exams or exams for advancement from grade to grade? What, if any, are the controversies surrounding these tests?

3. What have been the effects of testing and accountability on classroom practices in your community? Is there evidence that they have enhanced

teaching practices, or conversely that they have made teaching more routine and drill-oriented?

4. According to state statistics, what has happened to test scores since 2001? What has happened to achievement gaps among different racial groups during this period? How do these results compare to those available from NAEP?

5. What have been the positions of teacher unions in your state and community on state accountability and on No Child Left Behind? On other high-stakes tests like exit exams? On value-added measures to judge or reward teachers?

Selected Readings

Au, W. (2009). *Unequal by design: High-stakes testing and the standardization of inequality.* New York: Routledge.

Carnoy, M., Elmore, R., & Siskin, L. (Eds.) (2003). *The new accountability: High schools and high-stakes testing.* New York: Routledge.

Linn, R. L. (2008). Educational accountability systems. In K. Ryan & L. Shepard (Eds.), *The future of test-based educational accountability.* New York: Routledge.

Madaus, G., Russell, M., & Higgins, J. (2009). *The paradoxes of high stakes testing: How they affect students, their parents, teachers, principals, schools, and society.* Charlotte, NC: Information Age Publishing, Inc.

National Research Council of the National Academies (2011). *Incentives and test-based accountability in education.* Washington, DC: The National Academies Press.

Nichols, S. L. & Berliner, D. C. (2007). *Collateral damage: How high-stakes testing corrupts America's schools.* Cambridge, MA: Harvard Education Press.

Rebell, M. A. & Wolff, J. R. (Eds.) (2009). *NCLB at the crossroads: Reexamining the federal effort to close the achievement gap.* New York: Teachers College Press.

Rosenberg, B. (2008). Betrayal of the standards vision. In K. Ryan & L. Shepard (Eds.), *The future of test-based educational accountability.* New York: Routledge.

Ryan, K. & Shepard, L. (Eds.) (2008). *The future of test-based educational accountability.* New York: Routledge.

Steele, C. (2010). *Whistling Vivaldi, and other clues to how stereotype affects us.* New York: W.W. Norton & Company.

Education and Racism

Future Directions

As we have argued throughout this book, racism is a complex set of practices and relations. Its future seems secure as racism takes on the appearance of permanency. Its past is certainly incontrovertible even if discussing its present is somewhat controversial. Indeed, it is no exaggeration to argue that racism was part of the creation of the United States. That the States was a united country is a convenient use of the term since slavery and the Jim Crow institutions that followed Emancipation prevented Blacks from partaking in its liberties, Indian land appropriation was a reality, and a series of laws affecting Latinos and Asian Americans made citizenship status abstract rather than concrete. What remains to be argued is how this tension-filled past continues and affects today's U.S. society, including its education system. There is strong evidence to argue that not only do shameful past events like enslavement influence African American social mobility today, but racial discrimination in various forms continues to limit the advancement of children of color.

While we acknowledge that communities of color face their own internal challenges, we have tried to be clear about the challenges they did not create for themselves. As it is reproduced and practiced in schools, structural racism is one of those areas. Minorities may participate in racism, by internalizing it, but they are its targets, not its creators. Not merely victims, since they possess the ability to self-reflect, produce their own contradictions, and act on their own behalf, racial minorities in education suffer racism's multi-dimensions. From curriculum to classroom comportment, they are at a disadvantage. That said, based on the evidence and arguments, it is also our understanding that racism is not a complete process and leaves room for educators' power to ameliorate it as part of the educational interaction, not separate from it.

Before any efforts to intervene in race relations can take place, a thoroughgoing analysis is warranted. That is, educational solutions are only as good as educators' ability to understand the problem at hand, to explain certain causal mechanisms that lead to predictable results, and to craft perspectives based on evidence and justifications that are sustainable. These kinds of deliberations are critical if we include analysis as part of sound pedagogy and policy creation. Ideally, an education around race and racism should be integrated into some facet of undergraduate education and pre-service teacher education courses. As novice teachers prepare for their undertaking, they should be clear-eyed about the racial challenges that lie ahead and create practices that are meaningful and effective.

Toward a Color-conscious Education

In the Introduction, we set the stage by calling attention to color-blindness as one of the common frames used to understand race in the United States. In California, Propositions 227 (1998) and 209 (1996) struck a blow to vulnerable student populations when the first compromised bilingual education and the second made affirmative action unlawful. Because of these trends, color-conscious teacher education or undergraduate training faces real challenges. Thus, we do not underestimate the shift from color-blindness to color-consciousness. Nevertheless, race literacy is the educational ability to make race legible, to become adept at understanding its machinations, and to forge race-based explanations and solutions. This process is not straightforward and may even be counterintuitive for many people. However, we have argued that there are leading questions and issues that may guide the process.

Based on the preceding chapters and to return to our themes, a color-conscious education includes:

* *Curriculum:* Multiculturalism represents the most comprehensive reform of school knowledge that educators have witnessed since the mid-1980s. We emphasize its links with anti-racism. Inserting perspectives of color into the curriculum means that they are central to the understanding of history, the arts, and the construction of knowledge. It is decidedly cognizant of race and represents a platform to encourage diversity in schools. This is not done only for the benefit of students of color, but

also White or mainstream students, whose perspective is broadened and seen through the prism of racial difference, particularly through minority experiences.

• *Cultural Relevance:* A culturally relevant education is antithetical to color-blindness, making the worldview of families of color legitimate experiences on which to base classroom pedagogy. It necessitates questioning the apparently culture- or race-free interactions; instead, they stem from a "cultural arbitrary" disguised as universal culture. After locating this common culture, educators examine its language or discourse patterns to demystify its claims to universality. Minority groups' language practices do not supplant it as the new standard, but become part of an attempt to expand the cultural repertoire of a classroom, thereby expanding what it means to succeed as a student.

• *School–Community Relations:* Communities are not islands unto themselves. They exist as part of a network of relations with other communities. In many U.S. cities, suburban neighborhoods, for example, are products of White flight and were deliberately built for these reasons. As a result of this housing segregation, school segregation intensifies. The funds of knowledge found in communities of color are buried underneath the pathologies projected onto them. Excavating them requires a revaluation of these communities driven by their cultural vantage point, not those imposed from a White perspective. This takes an appreciation of how race matters in education.

• *Tracking:* Where an educator finds an interracial campus, he or she also finds the prominence of tracking. This practice is almost universal. On the face of it, tracking practices may increase efficiency by sorting students, often students differentiated racially, but justified by apparently race-neutral considerations like grades, and counselor and teacher recommendations. But evidence suggests that far from being free from racial bias, tracking complements it. In addition to funding disparities, tracking remains one of the most accepted practices that produces predictable racial outcomes. It tends to reinforce the century-old, now largely discredited, relationship between race and intelligence (IQ), this time returning under the banner of "ability grouping." Even if tracking creates efficiencies, which might be arguable, the racial costs of tracking are high. Heterogeneous grouping, or de-tracking, disrupts this practice by creating racially integrated classrooms and dispersing tracking's race-based outcomes.

- *Resources and Funding:* Funding is often the silver bullet in education reform discourse. Funnel more monies into struggling schools and improvements should result. There is some wisdom in this line of thought, since money clearly matters, but a broader argument about resources takes educators toward considering what race-based deficiencies, such as poor regard toward communities of color, hinder reform. Determining the funds of knowledge that remain to be tapped, like the cultural or community wealth of people of color, remains to be seen. These changes do not always take more money, but rather different perspectives.

- *Testing and Accountability:* Testing is touted as reliable when it is a valid instrument for measuring students' actual intelligence or mastery of a subject area and knowledge base. In addition, testing is said to be free of racial bias when tests consistently record a racial group's performance across different conditions of space and time. In other words, the tests' resemblance to race-based knowledge must be purged. On some level, testing is the ultimate litmus for color-blindness. It is education free of any vestige of race. However, tests are not outside a racialized society's confines, as evidenced by the scientific era of intelligence testing earlier in the 20th century and findings that standard tests, like the SAT and other entrance examinations, retain cultural bias. More often than not, tests reflect race turned into a knowledge relation. As a national educational agenda, the turn to standardized testing reflects the racial nature of academic ranking when it fails to account for individuals' racial experience in and out of schools.

As we suggest in Chapters 1–6, color-consciousness is the ability to understand how race matters in students' daily lives. It sounds strange to appropriate the very logic used to stratify education as a way to think through the problem, all the while avoiding reproducing its pitfalls, turning race from wood to stone. Not an easy hat trick. That is, just as we argued in Chapter 5 that it is imperative for educators to know when money matters, they should also know when race matters, or at least matters most critically in order to attest to its power. An example might show what we mean by this.

In an interview with Charlie Rose, Sean "Puffy" Combs, a famous and successful hip hop producer, was asked if racism had produced a ceiling for his success. Combs answered by stating that he was a very successful artist and businessman by any racial standard, White or Black. In effect, the suggestion was that Rose made too much of race. Combs's response does not suggest that there is no racism in the music industry; rather, Rose's question was the wrong one to ask. He was right to remind Rose that racism's glass ceiling was not the correct topic to broach in light of Combs's success that surpasses most businessmen of any color. Rose made too much of racism.

In another, unrelated interview, Matt Lauer of *Good Morning America* asked Halle Berry, an Oscar-winning actress, during the height of her career, if she had transcended racism, after achieving stardom and, we should add, the generally, if informally, acknowledged status of one of the most beautiful women of her time. Berry answered by reminding Lauer of the many leading roles that she was denied, which recalls the long-standing discrimination that Black artists have historically faced in Hollywood. In short, Lauer made too little of racism.

Aiming racial analysis at the "sweet spot," not falling below by underestimating it, and not rising above by exaggerating it, is easier said than done. That established, it is an ideal that is worthwhile for educators to consider. It does not guarantee that teachers will not commit the dreaded *faux pas*, as Rose and Lauer have shown us, but through self-reflection, teachers practice race awareness as part of a developmental process. It is the educative part of learning color-consciousness, where anti-racism is not a destiny, but a process.

As teachers hone their skill of race awareness, they understand the recursive relationship between practicing and reflecting upon race. Race is not just something we make, but something that makes us. This means that educators bring their racial histories into situations of practice, avoiding the problematic notion that they can begin anew by merely thinking anew. The practice–reflection circle requires that practice around race be conducted reflectively and remain open to criticism so that pedagogues, particularly Whites, understand it as a process rather than an end product. As a result, they avoid celebrating having reached the nirvana of race awareness once and for all. Or to put it colloquially, "If you think you got it, then you ain't got it." Race awareness is a process of becoming rather than being, a matter of practice rather than an identity one takes on. In other words, race awareness is what you do, not what you are.

Troubling Race

Race is both familiar and strange. As becomes obvious on most school campuses, students, if not also teachers, congregate by race. Educators need to look no further than the cafeteria, where young people sit together along racial lines (Tatum, 1997). Grouping by race is very familiar to Americans and it may seem natural to follow suit. Social tastes, friendship circles, and daily habits are informed by an invention turned into a reality. It is outside the scope of this book to question whether or not the United States should continue being a racialized nation (Leonardo, 2011). That would be a longer discussion and a more involved conversation around pedagogy. However, as educators go forward with a critical understanding of race, it is appropriate to unsettle some of its long-held practices and assumptions, to make it strange. That is, educators might consider troubling race.

For instance, race-as-biology has now been replaced with race-as-social-construction. Whereas in previous eras, race was understood as part of one's biological make-up, which made arguments around eugenics possible, like the link between race and intelligence, race is now understood as a product of social process rather than immutable laws of genetics. This means that rather than being a natural fact, educators invest race with meaning, particularly through the sheer repetition of stories about it. From the classroom to boardroom, race is filled with meaning through our rituals and practices. In other words, we (re)invent race every time we think or act through it. Schools are not an exception as race has become an intimate part of schooling. But rather than occurring generally, racialization happens in institutionally specific ways. We have outlined at least six of these practices in schools.

Testifying to race's influence on our lives also entails the danger of giving it even more meaning, indeed more power, than it already has. It begins to saturate every part of our social existence—it arguably already has. We may go a long way with asserting that reality has become racialized, but we find it useful to practice critical self-reflection around what race relations have made of us that we no longer consent to, such as their tendency to place limitations on our self-concept, interrelationships, and possible directions for civil development. They begin to take on a permanent status, both as a relation projected back into the past and well into the future. As it stands, race has no seeming beginning or foreseeable ending. But an education that makes the familiar strange questions the taken-for-granted aspects of schooling.

As the Introduction indicates, race is not a synonym for "social group." There are other social groups, for example, defined by ethnicity or nationality and the social conflicts they produce. The English treatment of the Irish retains some resemblance to racialization, as does anti-Semitism, both of which are deplorable and continue to this day with the fight for the independence of the former and vigilance against the latter. But within a U.S.-specific understanding of race, they are different from the Black–White binary or White–minority history. In this book, we have tried to illuminate race as the color line, which is an invention but produces real consequences nonetheless. That being established, the end of race as a social relation is more difficult to predict or imagine.

This last section of the book reminds educators of the active nature of racialization and asks them to keep in mind their participation in its processes even as they become critically aware of them. It is not a relation that is made once and for all, but one that people make over and over again. From choosing school class presidents (therefore who is smart or popular), to homecoming queens (therefore who is beautiful), to targets of disciplinary policies (therefore who is the troublemaker), race is part of how schools perceive students. Ultimately, race is learned, which makes it social, but not all aspects of it may be justifiable and sustainable. It behooves educators to understand which parts of race are worth keeping and which parts are not helpful. As it is, it is hard to imagine parts of education that are not touched by race.

Race awareness has its share of difficulties, including the residual biological, rather than social, explanations of race that remain in circulation. Although there is something biological in racial difference, such as those aspects expressed in phenotypical and other differences, by and large, race is a social concept invented to stratify society and its institutions, including schools. Also, racism is not an uncontroversial topic in schools and broaching it usually brings out tensions. Promoting color-consciousness in schools must be accomplished in a reflective and self-critical manner in order to avoid transforming its unreal parts, such as the biological rationale, into a social fact. Fortunately, there are many advocates and much academic work toward this end. This book may be considered as an effort to join those forces. As much as race and racism are part of the educational project, so is anti-racism. Its preliminary stages require thoughtful and careful analysis. Its enactment is a question for history, but one for the making rather than speculation.

Selected Readings

Leonardo, Z. (2011). After the glow: Race ambivalence and other educational progrnoses. *Educational Philosophy and Therapy, 43*(6), 675–698.

Tatum, B. D. (1997). *Why are all the Black kids sitting together in the cafeteria?* New York: Basic Books.

Index

Taylor & Francis

eBooks

FOR LIBRARIES

ORDER YOUR FREE 30 DAY INSTITUTIONAL TRIAL TODAY!

Over 23,000 eBook titles in the Humanities, Social Sciences, STM and Law from some of the world's leading imprints.

Choose from a range of subject packages or create your own!

Benefits for **you**

▶ Free MARC records
▶ COUNTER-compliant usage statistics
▶ Flexible purchase and pricing options

Benefits for your **user**

▶ Off-site, anytime access via Athens or referring URL
▶ Print or copy pages or chapters
▶ Full content search
▶ Bookmark, highlight and annotate text
▶ Access to thousands of pages of quality research at the click of a button

For more information, pricing enquiries or to order a free trial, contact your local online sales team.

UK and Rest of World: **online.sales@tandf.co.uk**

US, Canada and Latin America:
e-reference@taylorandfrancis.com

www.ebooksubscriptions.com

ALPSP Award for BEST eBOOK PUBLISHER 2009 Finalist

Taylor & Francis **eBooks**
Taylor & Francis Group

A flexible and dynamic resource for teaching, learning and research.